# YOU CAN'T FLY WITH THAT!

## Confessions of a Disgruntling Airport Security Officer

# Anonymous

ALL NAMES HAVE
BEEN CHANGED

# INTRO

W e've all been there.

You hit snooze one too many times, or traffic was slow, or you couldn't find your house key ... and just like that, you're late for your flight. Now, passport and boarding pass in hand, you're nearly there. You can almost taste that Mexican margarita, or feel the snow beneath your skis.

There's one last, formidable thing standing between you and your hard-earned vacation and the first dreaded hint of what's in store comes in the form of an endless, snaking line of travellers, shuffling—just like you—dejectedly towards a gloomy, grey mirage of conveyer belts and monolithic metal detectors punctuated by sagging, lopsided towers of scuffed, grey plastic bins. Those two dreaded words that chill the blood of even the most seasoned frequent flyer: airport security: the necessary scourge of modern air travel. That unavoidable obstacle in your journey out of Dodge; likely to forcefully relieve you of forgotten water bottles, expensive face cream and—more often than not—any last remaining shreds of dignity.

Yes, yes ... you and I both know you couldn't hide a home-made explosive in the foamy sole of your well-worn Nike, even if you wanted to, but unfortunately, a petty criminal named Richard Reid tried to ignite his kicks on a flight back in 2001, so now we're all obliged to take off our shoes before taking to the skies. (Yes, for the hundredth time, your flip flops come off too, Sir ... sigh). So here we are. I'm forced to dig through your underwear because you somehow forgot about that litre of Fiji water; or I'm making you march back and forth through the metal detector, methodically stripping you of jewellery and coins like a pickpocket, until you finally remember there's a smartphone in your pocket. And *you're* ... miserable.

Have you ever thought about what it's like to work the security line at an international airport as your full-time job? No, of course you haven't. Just like you haven't pondered the exquisite joys of manning the counter of your local DMV or dreamed of working the lines at a big customer support call centre. Why? Because, in each of these cases you're not dealing with relaxed, happy people but rather individuals who are frustrated, impatient, anxious or—despite your best efforts—wilfully clueless. As for you—the employee—you're viewed as a human roadblock; a nuisance; nothing more than a means to an end, whether it be a new licence or a refund or, in my case, that precious flight for which you're running late (which, in case you'd forgotten, is your fault, not mine!).

In any case, it takes a special kind of person to work a job like mine. You need the patience of a saint, amongst a host of other characteristics shared by only the most even-keeled, perpetually unflappable individuals. However, if you can learn to steel yourself against the monotony and the near-constant frustration, there's a virtually untapped reservoir of humour up for grabs ...

# ENTER THE MADNESS

Dishevelled and overwhelmed, you enter the security checkpoint. You pat your pockets for the fiftieth time in the past hour, circling back around to the front, unsure if the initial check was thorough enough. Passports have been known to commit suicide, leaping to their deaths out of boredom.

A twenty-nine-year-old Asian male with spiky hair, professional in dress, methodically directs you to the left with a lazy point of his finger. That's Ho, and in eight hours he'll be sitting next to me in his Dodge. After a long haul on his weed vape pen, he'll turn to me and say, "Did you see Margot Robbie come through today? Mannnnn, she's hot. Lululemon? Are you serious, Margot? Are you trying to get me written up for having a hard-on. Give me a break."

Next, you'll arrive at Armando, a white thirty-year-old, who looks kind, but sure isn't. He'll scan your boarding pass and wish you a nice flight. Three days earlier, on Saturday night,

Armando and I heard a banging on the bathroom stall we were sharing at the club. A large, seemingly straight bouncer sternly began with, "Hey, what are you two doing in there? It better not be drugs" However, once I open the door, he changed his tune and suggested more softly, "Or if it's sex, can I join?" We weren't having sex. He got drugs.

In the same club, on the same night, Jazz, a frumpy thirty-three-year-old Indian with a cool do, could be found slurping spilled tequila off the bar top, in an area manufactured as our VIP section. Now, at the checkpoint divest station, he'll ask you to take out your laptops, liquids, gels and aerosols. If he's not too stoned, he might even ask you to remove your shoes. That's a big if.

Approaching the metal detector, you'll spot a female screening officer, leaning up against the x-ray machine on the other side. Maybe she's using the cancer causer as support, because she's exhausted from chasing after her two small children, both under five; or she may still be suffering the effects of a concussion I facilitated the night before. As a thank you for helping me stuff my couch's parts into their slip covers, I offered mouth service, tongue twisting an eventual shake to the floor, and her noggin gave my coffee table a head-high-five on the way past.

Lastly, rocking a fresh-pressed suit, you'll notice Max standing at a podium in front of a laptop. He may look professional, however, in a few months he'll be getting his face swallowed by a recently-dumped British girl on Koh San Road, Bangkok, only minutes before jet-puking on a gate that separates him from government buildings' housing men, willing to shoot him in the dome for such offences. He's the person to whom you can hand written complaints about me. Next to him is a garbage can. That's where those complaints end up. Enjoy your flight.

# GENESIS

"Can I go pee?" asked Peter, a frail Sri Lankan of about twenty-five, from somewhere over my shoulder. The question startled me from a night-time daydream. Is that a thing? I was having a daydream, but during a night-shift. Night-dream? That's too confusing. My head was somewhere else.

"Peter, I know you *can* go to the washroom, because you do it about fifty times a night. You want permission to use the washroom? Or as you so eloquently put it, go pee. You're an adult and I'm not your babysitter. I've told you many times, some of them tonight even, that if you need to use the washroom, just go. I'm very busy."

The screen open on my computer was for my fantasy basketball lineup. I minimized it, bringing forward a work spreadsheet I barely understood. Its sole purpose was to hide an open email, Facebook, and job search page.

Peter just stood there, dumbfounded; his default setting.

Exasperated, I sighed and said, "Just go to the washroom." As he scuttled away, I yelled after him, "And for the last time, don't ask again."

Peter is a dummy. Someone so dumb, he'd soon key my silver Volkswagen Passat in a well-lit parking lot, overlooked by hundreds of visible surveillance cameras; hours after I laid him off for redundancy, and for having the memory retention of a concussed goldfish.

Kind-hearted as I am, I declined to involve the cops, although, as retaliation, I kept his sister and girlfriend employed, knowing that neither of them had a driver's license. That required Peter to chauffeur them. I considered the inconvenience a charity, providing him job experience in one of the only few fields he was intellectually qualified to work.

I didn't enjoy condescendingly deconstructing the nuanced grammar of "can" versus "may". Nor did I later enjoy firing people because of downsizing (with obvious exceptions). However, one can only labour among the machines for so long, before becoming a cog. That's exactly what I'd begun to hate about myself. Because of this, I'd started to click job postings requiring less responsibility and, more importantly, involving fewer phone calls in the middle of my days off, asking what to do when a computer froze; Alt+control+delete, moron. Alt. Control. Delete.

Peter came back from his washroom break twenty-minutes later and, in his quiet, breathless, elderly man-fashion, asked "When's break?" In my head, I bashed his dumb face with my keyboard. In reality, I swivelled my chair to separate us and sighed. Then I reluctantly offered screen name, Hoopboy6969, Kobe Bryant for Dwight Howard, in a desperate need to beef up my rebound and block categories. Break was at the exact same minute every day.

Where other friends my age, with similar titles to mine, had sought career advancements, I pined for demotions. This is more problematic than you'd think. Evidently, it's more difficult to get a job you're overqualified for, than under. Conclusively, lying is easier when you're falsely promoting yourself.

At first, the role with a major phone company had seemed perfect: Lead, work hard when I wanted, and I was in charge. Overall, it satisfied my objection to authority, because I was the authority, answerable only to a bunch of suits who were intimidated by my mild, unexplained success and angst-filled attitude. Eventually though, the anxiety and constant demand wore on me.

I grew up with a mom who often told me, "If you don't like a job, make it fun. If you get fired from that job; then good, get another you enjoy." The philosophy became my work mantra. I used a similar approach to girlfriends. Not exactly what my kind, religious mom had in mind, but hey, don't hate the player, hate the game

About three weeks into my search, and a few months before my severance package kicked in, I found a job that met my prerequisites. The government was hiring security screeners for a nearby international airport. Pay: good. Physical exertion: minimal. Most importantly, the role demanded nothing of me after hours. Oh, and add to that a union for protection, publicly-perceived power and, most importantly, no more wearing a suit. I had applied with little hope, seeing myself as someone who was not very, "stoppy stop, terrorism-esque."

Against all expectations, I heard back soon after applying for the airport screener job. I got the call and answered questions for about thirty minutes. As I sat next to my employees for the duration of the call, it was evident to them all that I no longer gave a damn, or knew what one was to give it – shout out, Eminem.

I responded, "Tuesday won't be a problem," to the HR rep's question of, "Does Tuesday work?" A long silence filled the conversation. Had he hung up? Died?

"Hello?" I asked, "You still there?"

There was a fumbling of phone, then, "Yes, sorry. I thought maybe you were still talking."

Shaking my head and puffing my cheeks frustrated, I replied, "No, that was it. Tuesday works. Is there anything important I should know?"

"Nope."

"Anything I should bring?"

"Nope."

"Okay."

Fifty seconds more of silence. Were we playing a game?

"Yep," he provided. It wasn't even his most useless contribution to our call. The conversation was beginning to feel like the awkward ones I'd had with girlfriends when I was trying to break up, but was too much of a pussy to pull the trigger.

"See you then," I offered, in an attempt to put an end the call.

"Oh no, I won't be there."

You're killing me here, man.

I thought, "Too bad. We've created what I think will be an unbreakable, lifelong friendship here."

I said, "I see. Well, thanks for calling. Take care."

Throughout the chat, he had spoken slowly and methodically, like someone had typed words into a machine and it was reciting them. Anticipating the end of our call, he rapidly spat out, "I forgot to mention, you'll need ... " into the phone, listing off a good fifteen vital instructions, that if I didn't follow would have me showing up looking like a eunuch's condom.

# THE INTERVIEW

Scrolling through the job posting for Airport Screening Officer, a few things caught my eye—or, to be exact, the absence of things did.

- *Competency with technology.*
- *Accountability for one's own actions and decisions.*
- *Fluency in English, spoken and written.*

Was I applying to play the role of a seven-year-old?

Logically, if you're reading the ad, you automatically must possess some competency with technology. I mean, maybe you were spastically smashing your jibs off the ol' QWERTY and fatefully pulled up a job-listing board, but most likely you competently technologized your way over to the post. As if reaching the page wasn't evidence enough of your skills, you managed to scroll down to the bottom and clicked on the Apply button—a sure sign of competency.

The thing with showing accountability for one's own actions and decisions is, first you must place yourself in a situation where this is required. A simple case of, don't put the cart before the horse. They must have given up on the third prerequisite. By the time I applied, the companies average was at best fifty percent.

The only real prerequisite that wasn't particularly perceptive was: Graduated high school. Becoming a terrorist requires a more scrupulous applicant. Have you seen where some of those guys live? No wonder they're rushing to get into heaven. Forget ninety virgin wives; I'm pretty sure they'd settle for a place with reliable electricity and spotty WI-FI, anything a little less ... 'cavey'.

I went to high school with a guy who was suspended multiple times for walking around with his dick hanging out of his open fly; he graduated. Is this is all airport security required? I felt that a job that existed to stop airplane-related terrorism should have higher standards, maybe a fitness or psych test, at least something that would dissuade employees from walking around with their knobs loose, flapping dangerously close to the airplane propellers.

I nervously prepared for my interview, adjusting my tie in the mirror while reciting answers to questions I thought I might be asked. My roommate, Gary, stopped at my door and watched me for a second. Then he asked, "You want my help? I'm an excellent interviewer."

I squinted, processing his request. I replied, "You work for yourself and have done so for like seven years. Before that, you worked with me, at a place that hires ex-convicts. Where'd you learn these excellent interview skills?"

"In school."

"Why'd you have interviewing in school? You took poly-sci."

Unperturbed by my inquiry, he continued, shrugging off

my question. "So, first you need to know that it's important to ask the interviewer more questions than they ask you."

"That doesn't seem right at all."

Ignoring me further, he continued. "That way, they'll know you're playing hardball."

"I'm not trying to play hardball. They pay a set hourly wage. It's non-negotiable. Where do you think I'm trying to work?"

"It's all the same man. They want to know you're tough, that you won't be walked all over."

"The job listing said the most important quality to have is customer service. What you're saying is kinda the opposite of that."

"Neither here nor there my man. Toughness, that's the name of the game."

"Are you high?"

"Very."

I dismissively flicked my wrist then shooed him away with, "Get out of here, horn licker."

In my previous job with the phone company, I'd been referred by a friend, which avoided an interview and jumped me right into orientation. Not that it really counted as one, but the last real interview I actually had was in Australia, five years earlier. Even that resembled a date more closely than an interview. While living in Sydney, I'd applied for a job giving poker seminars. Shortly after I sent in the online application, I received a call from a man asking if I wanted to meet in a pub, in an hour, to see if I fit with his company. Three hours later I was loaded on Heineken, had a job and had made a friend who used the 'C-word' as a verb, noun, adverb, and adjective. Needless to say, I was out of practice at interviewing.

I arrived for my interview dressed in a slick suit, and prepared for a thorough meeting. In hindsight, I don't think it would have mattered if I'd showed up in a children's Winnie the Pooh costume. In a sparse office foyer located in the airport's underbelly, I was met by Julio, a snowman-shaped fella with one functioning hand. I reached out to shake. He withdrew a dwarfed, frozen-chicken wing and awkwardly cupped his left hand over my outstretched right. Great, as if I'd be able to take my eyes off a deformed arm. We were off to a good start.

Next, he had me fill out a small questionnaire of five questions, more or less asking me things on the resume I'd just handed him. I finished in three minutes. Five minutes of waiting time grew to ten and ten led to me considering leaving the small, windowless office to fetch him. I didn't, worrying that somehow he'd slip in without us seeing each other and think I'd left, confused by questions which had no correct or incorrect answer. Instead, I began rolling my thumbs, until I thought, "What if he's watching and thinks I'm ridiculing his inability to perform the act?"

I actually thought that. I'm such a prick.

Thirty minutes later, he returned panting. Not surprising, considering. His frumposaurus-rex stature wheezed that he was someone who'd go into cardiac arrest just saying the word cardio. Short of breath, he asked, "Are you finished yet?" My jaw reflectively unhinged, facilitating my mouth into saying something sarcastic. I needed a job though, so kept it shut, for once. In my head, I thought, "He was definitely taking a crap. He's a guy who takes a lot of craps."

Again, I'm such a prick.

A deep breath away from an asthma attack, he said, "I'm going to ask you a few questions," and went on to read me the five questions from the questionnaire I had just filled out.

Ashton Kutcher? Where are you hiding?

"I have one last question. It has no bearing on you getting the job. Is that okay?"

I responded, "Shoot."

Maybe not the best response given the job had a lot to do with preventing exactly that from happening.

"Do you believe in aliens?"

I noticed his wing twitch, presumably because his brain dictated it meet his other hand for a devious finger-steepling, Monty Burns-style. Unfortunately, Chicken Little's role was re-signed to stiff lingering and couldn't perform the feat. I answered his question confidently.

"In my experience, the only things people ask you if you believe in, have never been proven real. I'm yet to come across someone who asks me whether I believe the ocean, sun, or they are real. Although, I'd definitely welcome someone asking me if they were real. It'd demonstrate they had some big philosophical balls, ready to be shown. Neither has happened, however, leading me to believe that anything that is so far-fetched that people go around asking others if they believe in it, doesn't exist. That all being said, show me proof of something and I'm open-minded to admitting it exists."

I'd gone off the cuff, spoken out of my dirt star. I wasn't really sure if what I'd said made any sense or not. To be fair, that has never stopped me before and I certainly wasn't going to let it stop me during an interview of all places. I assumed that any normal person, who'd ask that particular question during an interview, was either an expert on the topic, ready to preach their own theory the moment you stopped talking, or a complete idiot.

"Good answer," he responded as he finished up with the only notes he'd taken the whole interview, proving he was the latter: a complete idiot.

"We'll let you know when we've made a decision."

I wondered if the decision had to do with the alien debate or the job.

# LAYOVER

I found out a few days after the interview that I'd made it to the next stage of hiring. The call came from the same HR smuck who'd contacted me for the interview, and went just about as well.

"Okay, so you'll want to be dressed nicely for your training, that's important."

Eager, I asked enthusiastically, "What exactly do you mean by nice? Suit and tie?"

"No, no," he said dismissively. "Not that nice."

Apparently, it was time to play a guessing game.

"Dress shirt and pants?"

"Probably something more like that, yeah."

Would I look like a dick if I asked, "Probably like that, or exactly like that?"

Time to find out.

"Probably like that or exactly like that?"

"Yeah, wear something nice and you'll be okay."

I was exasperated. If I was ten, I'd have handed the phone over to my mom and said, "Please deal with this." But, I wasn't ten, I was a grown man. Wait. What's that in Gary's hand? I covered the phone's mic. "Gary, are you eating my Dinosaur fruit snacks? I'll kill you, you dinkwad, homo." I smacked them from his hand, raining down Brontosaurus's and T-Rex's on our hardwood floor. Yet another extinction dealt to those poor sauruses.

I asked the worst HR guy in the world, "Any particular colour of nice clothes?"

"Go light."

I thought-screamed, "BLOWS IN THE WIND, LIGHT? YOU MORON. WHITE? BEIGE? AM I DRESSING LIKE I'M GOING TO CHURCH AFTER LABOUR DAY? SPIT IT OUT, SPASTIC!!!!!"

I resigned myself to bringing eight outfits.

"Thanks for calling. I'll see you ..." I cut myself off, avoiding the same mistake I'd made last time. "Take care."

"No problem. I'll see you in a few months at your training."

Ahhhhhhhh!!!!!

I had about four months to kill, in between the phone company giving me severance and waiting for my airport security clearance and training. To pass the time and to ensure that my money wasn't squandered in dramatic flicks of bills towards naked females with daddy issues, serving up lappers to pay for college, I worked a few days here and there helping friends with their businesses. I picked up some writing gigs, and, unfortunately, worked a two-week stint in which I played a 'brain dead numbskull', yanking car parts out of a furnace for a tool-and-die company.

With Gary off for the winter, only a few months until

I started at the airport, and a wallet bursting with severance package Benjamin's, I soon succumbed to Gary's constant texts of, "Let's do something fun," and gave up slaving for the man to entertain my boy.

"Something fun," to Gary, always included booze.

Soul mates.

Gary's character in a movie would be listed in the closing credits as, Lazy Slacker. He'd have five lines and all would include him saying "Dude" at least once, and end with him taking either a sip of beer or a pull from a joint. Unfortunately, Gary isn't reliable or ambitious enough to have ever made it outta bed and to the audition so he continued to mooch off his parents, his girlfriends, and work as a one-man, interlocking landscaper, qualified through the university of YouTube tutorials.

It didn't matter whether I asked Gary at 3:00 a.m. or p.m., "Wanna grab a drink?" The answer was always either, "Yep, I'll grab my shoes.", "Yes. Meet you there now. I'm sitting at the bar." or, "I'm on a date. Meet you there in an hour."

This lifestyle seemed to contrast that of which I imagined an airport security guard should be living. Shouldn't I be practising straightening a tie in a bathroom mirror? Holding my arm up in a halt gesture? Condescendingly shaking my head 'no'?

As it turns out, no. None of that mattered at all. Fast forward three months and the x-ray machine, which I'd previously presumed facilitated the defence of our public, was primarily playing the role of physical supporter, holding me up when I'm too hungover to stand.

# TRAINING

**M**uch as how, according to R. Kelly, after the party is the hotel lobby, after the interview is all the dang training. Unlike R. Kelly, my training group didn't marry or pee on underage girls, at least not that I know of; maybe I was left out of the fun. We did, however, suffer through the melancholy drone of a less than enthusiastic Big Brother trainer (Big Brother is what I'll be referring to the governing body throughout the book, except for right now, where I'm referring to them as the governing body). The monotonous recitation of things such as, "And one more time, what are the non-permitted items again?"

"Guns and bombs, Clare. Geeze. We get it. We're post 9/11 here. If you can't bring it into a Chucky Cheese, you can't bring it on a plane. It isn't that damn hard."

It became obvious after day one, there was going to be a lot of filler. Clare could've easily wrapped the whole thing up in eight hours, no problem. The only thing stopping her was an al-

lotted training budget designated for a week. It was not dissimi-
lar to the way a paving company knocks off a home driveway in
three hours, but takes three months to do the same size one for a
city contract.

The isolated room, humming from the overhead lights
and computers only permissible to touch during tests – you absolutely cannot use it to check Facebook. Say that all you want
but I don't think you were joking – was windowless and stuck
dead center of the airport. Half of our break was spent finding
our way through a maze of halls that, with luck and assistance,
lead to the public area. By the time we escaped the labyrinth,
—but not before going down five halls, we were quickly told
we weren't allowed in—break was over. We were left shovelling
sandwiches and granola bars down our gullets while high-step-
ping it back. I tried to avoid vagrant mustard from escaping its
bread jail and plopping onto my white shirt, which out of the
lack of me owning any other white dress shirts, and my being required to wear a white dress shirt only every day, needed to stay
fresh and condiment free. Unavoidable blemishes were worn
like badges, an indication of how many meals, therefore, days,
we'd lasted in training.

On Wednesday, midway through the in-class training, I
was feeling a bit dejected. I got home around seven and plopped
down next to Gary, my sigh matching the deflation of fart air
harboured in the pleather couch cushion. Gary removed his
right hand from his pants and placed it on my thigh, before saying mock-sympathetically, "Why so glum, chum? Training got
you down? Wanna quick handy?"

I swept his hand from my leg, and responded, "Ugh, get
your dick mitten away from me; and, too many questions. I'm
drained."

"Awww, come on buddy. What's the 411 over there at the
port of air? You stopping terrorism yet?"

He didn't think I was ever going to be stopping terrorism,
any more than I did. In fact, when told him I'd gotten the job,

he'd gone as far as scouring the internet to find articles and videos containing airport security mishaps, followed by an investigative report on its secondary role next to counterintelligence, a department articulately described in this metaphor: A tractor-trailer truck pulling a bike behind it. I lived with Gary for over a year and not once did he go grocery shopping or make his bed. Apparently, his efforts were reserved for demoralizing me and tricking girlfriends into drinking a coffee containing hidden chlamydia meds.

"It's a joke. If I ask a reasonable question about a hole in our security or SOP, it's – ***COMPANY SECRET*COMPANY SECRET*** – nonsense. Not - ***COMPANY SECRET***-. Not – **COMPANY SECRET***-. Today, I think I actually saw my trainer look at one of the security cameras in the room. As if she was acknowledging, to the person watching on the other end, that I might know too much already."

Gary asked, "Did the secret service follow you home afterwards and go through your trash? You're sounding like your ex now."

I fake laughed then replied, "Funny. We were told that liquids over 100 ml are confiscated and thrown away. You're borderline spazzy and I bet you have the same question as me. Go."

Gary took a second, and then responded, "Can 101 ml blow up a plane better than 100? Isn't placing a bomb in a garbage-can next to you stupid? Don't you have a machine to test if it is a bomb? Don't bombs look like they do in Road Runner cartoons, say TNT and are easy to spot?"

I nodded slowly, sucking my teeth while saying, "You got it. And when *I* said that, do you know what the trainer said?"

"Good questions. Now I'll answer?"

I switched my head movement to side-to-side, and corrected Gary with, "She said: that's not part of the training. Then remorselessly went on to say how important greeting the passenger with the SOP standard greeting is to customer service.

I looked around the room and my ten classmates avoided eye-contact and seemed oblivious to my logic."

Gary cut short his role in our conversation, offering a departing, "You know they're going to implant a tracking device in you soon, right?"

I retaliated, "Now who's schizo?" as we instinctively sprang from the couch and headed towards the door, destined for the pub.

When it came time to do the tests at the end of the week, I breezed through them. Questions such as, "What do you do if you see someone sweating a lot, acting shady, constantly looking around, and saying I'm going to blow this bitch up?" didn't even have a space to fill in an answer. We were given four multiple choice options:

1. Nothing

2. Cry

3. Nothing

4. Alert your supervisor that there's a man acting suspiciously. Follow your SOP's.

Lulling over the brain-buster, I caught Doug, sitting next to me, peaking at my screen. I vowed to bid for opposite shifts as him and never to fly when he was scheduled.

On the first day of training I'd come in holding a pad of paper and replacement pens, nervous about what lay ahead. By day five, I was getting - **\*MY SECRET\*** - before class with Andy, another person in my hiring group, concerned about nothing other than what Subway's sub of the day was. I was nostalgic about replacing the LCD screen on a 2017 model, something I never thought possible. The divide between my romanticized profession and reality grew vaster with every boring word that came out of Clare's mouth.

I tried the concerns I'd given Gary on Andy. "Do you notice how Clare brushes off any difficult question I have? I'm addressing holes that make terrorism easier and she doesn't seem to care. Like has no one ever – *COMPANY SECRET*COMPANY SECRET* - How are we ignoring that that could happen?"

He shrugged indifferently. I continued with, "And if we suspect someone is … - *COMPANY SECRET*COMPANY SECRET* - we just - *COMPANY SECRET* - and then - *COMPANY SECRET*? Why aren't we - *COMPANY SECRETING* - on the guy?"

"But it pays good," he responded. "And they give us dry-cleaning money."

I gave up. He'd obviously had his chip installed already.

Monday morning, our training group had consisted of fifteen people. By Friday, only five remained, two of whom were people redoing the training because of long absences, and were privy to the lessons and test answers. I have no idea how anyone failed. As I mentioned, the tests were easy. I passed and spent nearly every minute of class replaying my life, attempting to conjure the place I'd gone wrong, and not paying attention to a word. In fairness, my mental absenteeism is Clare's fault, culpable if only for doing a review of exactly what would be on the test, five seconds before the test. I stopped listening soon after I learned this.

I can honestly say, I learned less practical work knowledge in the forty-plus hours of training than I would have learned during ten minutes on the live line. Really, the only benefits of in-class training were meeting a few people in proximity to me on the company's employee seniority list. I planned on exhausting them as proxies for my shift and vacation bidding, when selections fell on days I wasn't scheduled to work.

I had this doozy of a conversation with one of the failers, a few minutes after class ended. He approached me at the classroom door. Clearly dejected, he sullenly offered, "Can you believe those bastards made the test so difficult?"

I scanned my exiting classmates, gauging whether any would bail me out of the conversation. I think they sensed what was going on; logical people avoid failures.

"Um, the test we just did?" I asked, attempting to buy time, still hoping to be saved.

"Yeah man. That was insane. Do you remember question four? Like how the hell would we know that?" He pushed on, undeterred by my indifference. Honestly, the most difficult question on the test was whether liquids were allowed, if they were for medical purposes. True or false to boot.

"Question four eh. Question four hmm," I childishly lulled over his comment.

Misinterpreting non-committal repetition as camaraderie, he excitedly proclaimed, "Yeah, you're with me. What other ones did you have trouble with?"

"Hmmmm, the one about threats?" I offered.

He smiled for the first time in our conversation, excited to have found someone who shared his troubles. He sprang into action suggesting, "Crap, yeah that one too. We should go complain together. Tell them it was too hard."

"Oh, no," I stuttered. "I've got some important stuff to take care of, like ..." I trailed off, unable or caring enough to make an excuse.

Dejected, he responded, "Ah, bummer. Thanks anyways, man. See ya in a bit," with his head down. Escaping as swiftly as my Zara Oxfords allowed, I sped-walked to meet my fellow passers. Our group grabbed a coffee (because unlike the failers, we had jobs and could afford them) then sat around a flimsy, stainless-steel table, talking about how easy the test was. About ten minutes later, the failer walked past. Pausing momentarily in front of our table, he shook his head in my direction and threw his arms up in sarcastic surrender. Then, thankfully he left. I'm assuming because his mom was there to pick him up.

Training taught me that professionalism and customer

service were the pinnacles of my obligations. With that in mind, I took the few days I had between finishing training and working my first live-line shift, to contemplate how someone possessing the two qualities conducted themselves, hoping to mimic the template until my three-month probation period was over; it wasn't going to be easy.

# A CHICKEN FOR YOUR TIME, GOOD SIR

**W**hat does a guy who's waited five months for his clearance pass, another couple of months for a training class, finished two weeks of excruciatingly boring training and tests, and is running cutting-coupon-low on funds, do the night before his very first shift? Go to a gosh-darn, kick-bum, mansion party on the lake, that's what.

I turned to Ron, large and in charge behind the wheel of his F-150 truck while en route to the party, and said, "I can't get that drunk tonight dude. I've got my first shift tomorrow at eleven. Is this going to be a big jamboree?"

Confusion creased his bald melon. He pondered while dirty laundered. Finally he questioned with, "What the blood clot are you even talking about?"

I asked, "Where am I losing you? It's jamboree, isn't it?"

"That's the one."

"Big party? Small party?" I rephrased.

"Ugh. I just told you, it's a mansion party. I went to a Halloween party here and the owner had escorts carrying around drinks and drugs. So ... big."

"Oh no, little guy, this is bad. I need to be on my best behaviour tomorrow. Why are you doing this to me?"

"Ugh."

"My sentiments exactly."

*At this point, a normal person may start feeling irresponsible about their life decisions.*

The party was as advertised. We walked in the front door and were greeted by a thirty-foot-wide, twenty-foot-tall fish tank. If my high school math is still serving me well, that equals ... a lotta water. Outside a gigantic kitchen littered with Texas mickey's of different alcohol, we saw an infinity pool dropping off into the lake. The rest of the backyard held more Texas mickeys, food, two hot tubs, a grotto, and countless people.

The owner brought my friends Ron, Stick and I into a large room with walls lined in cubbies filled with whisky. He asked, "You boys ever tried fifteen-thousand dollar whisky?" I doubt I've had a fifty dollar bottle. I shook my head, no. The other guys, both dressed as if they'd been dropped off after gym class, assumed the question was rhetorical and just stood there dumbfounded. I guessed it was going to taste magical. It didn't. It tasted like whisky. As tempting as it was to inform him that he'd been ripped off, I smiled and said, "Mmm, that's the stuff." "The stuff that makes me wish I had a chaser or no tongue," I thought.

*If the feeling of irresponsibility or remorse kicked in now, we'd be okay.*

We toured the rest of the house, pausing in a movie theatre, for some shots. Next to a car elevator holding a Rolls Royce, we paused for another shot, and then, at a bar bigger than most found at actual bars, for a shot. Then down a hidden hallway that led to a hidden room, where, you guessed it … we were all out of shots and had to stumble back upstairs.

*Still nada.*

It was probably somewhere around the tenth shot that I lost track of most memories. I have a vague recollection of making out with a girl in the theatre and another in a sauna. Big pimpin. It then skips either forward or backward to being outside in the grotto. Finally, it ends with me waking up, face down, in the neighbour's front yard.

*The point of no return. There's no chance of feeling feelings anymore. I know hungover/still drunk me.*

I searched my pockets and found my phone. Surprisingly, 9:35 a.m. filled the screen. I stumbled across the yard and up to Ron's truck. He was passed out in the front seat. I shook him awake. Now, there's no possible way that if he'd drunk even half as much as me he should've driven me to work, but he did. Why? Because he's a real trooper; and because I'm pretty sure the neighbours were eventually going to call the cops if I remained sprawled out across some billionaire's lawn. Ron took me to a coffee shop and we loaded up on "get-sober" carbs.

"What happened last night?" I asked.

He gave me the "Who me?" look. He asked, "Who me? I was going to ask you."

"Did we do drugs?"

"All the drugs."

"Okay, good. Glad to know we didn't waste any."

*There we go, finally, a hint of regret.*

We turtled the last stretch of airport driveway and pulled in front of the building just before eleven. Boy, oh boy I was still saaaaaaaa-mashed. With a few survivalist texts, I discovered a friend from my training class was working.

I texted Andy, "Please find a way so I don't have to work. I'm so hungover."

He wrote back right away, "Yeah, I know, I saw your Snapchats. You looked gone. I'll see what I can do."

I sat tight. Waiting, but also unable to functionally move. A few minutes later I received his reply.

"So the supervisor says if you buy him chicken for lunch he'll let you punch in and just chill in the lunchroom, until you feel better. Just bring it in with you. He wants fries on the side. Deal?"

I quickly wrote back, "Yes, duh," and remained slumped in the passenger seat for another twenty minutes, before I staggered into the building.

*A more accurate reflection of the future, impossible.*

My scheduled shift was from eleven to three. I entered the lunchroom just after eleven and left at three-thirty, sleeping past the end of my shift. Surprisingly, the supervisor and I became friends afterwards. He's since had many, many, free chicken lunches, thanks to me.

# WE HAVE LIFT OFF

In the weeks leading up to leaving my telephone gig, I'd verbally romanticized my new position at the airport and my
perceived benefits of it to my employees.

"The countdown to my freedom has begun you pecker-
heads," I manically spat through evil laughter while hovering
over my dejected phone elves. "Soon, I'll be kicking terrorist
in the dicks and buying discounted airport merchandise. Enjoy
unscrewing phones, suckas."

I couldn't have been more wrong.

Standing on the checkpoint floor, an hour into my slow-
moving, first shift, I observed my colleagues one by one. I
quickly grew empathetic towards pre-school teachers and Jerry
Springer. I became harshly aware that my problem-solving
skills and personality wouldn't be helpful in the North-Korea-
prison-camp environment of an airport checkpoint. Don't get
me wrong, once I got to know some of the same people I ori-

ginally thought were *One-Flew-Over-the-Cuckoo's-Nest-* post-op dull, I realized a lot of them were only temporally Pavlovian conditioned to be zombies. After all, airport security is a job of rules, restrictions, and most importantly, no questions (in Big Brother's opinion). How's a person to stay normal with that nonsense going on? I didn't blame them.

In a matter of only a few months, my job title changed drastically from, Senior Manager of Production and Efficiency at a major phone company, to Screening Officer; or, unofficially, 'Taker of Water from the Elderly'. I went from my employees bringing me coffee to passengers yelling at me for taking theirs. From having a free phone with unlimited everything, to being scolded like a child and then fired if I had my phone out on the line. From being, "Sir," to, "asshole, prick, mall cop, jerk-off, and loser;" And, on one occasion—my fav—"Cock twat."

I felt the downgrade immediately. Mind you, it didn't take much to get used to less responsibility, no early morning strategy calls and being asked, "Can I go to the washroom?" seven hundred times a night. Besides, if I'd stayed put, the alternative was working a shift I didn't want, with people I didn't like, in a city I didn't even like driving through. I settled into the airport, satisfied ... for the time being.

My friends knew I was aloof and my sudden downgrade in careers didn't really surprise them. This was weird, because *I* was surprised. Weren't adults supposed to long for prestigious positions? Affluence? Chedda? Over a month had passed and I was still hung up on the fact that my interviewer hadn't even batted an eye over me giving up managing a team of eight-hundred people, to carry bins to passengers. If I'd made the career change for shock-value, it hadn't worked.

New screening officers are eased into responsibility; given the more one-dimensional of the one-point-five-dimensional positions their first few weeks. On my second shift at the airport, I rotated to scanning. My role was to call people through a metal detector and if they set off the alarm, to ascertain what had triggered the annoying beep and resolve it. It was mindless work, often requiring hours of standing and either nodding or directing confused people through the narrow, rectangular entry. Absentmindedly picking up an empty, cardboard glove box, I ripped off one end. I jotted down some observations about my surroundings, mostly humorous reactions from passengers. I filled the paper and ripped another end, soon filling that. Twenty minutes later, I'd written on every inch of the inside of the box and was searching for another surface to write on.

I've been recording my life and work stories since I lived in Australia ten years ago, immortalizing my idiocy and sequential firings and pooed pants. Less than an hour into my shift in a security checkpoint, I knew I'd struck funny-story gold. Five years later, I haven't stopped writing.

Day one, a phone wasn't metal. Day two, toothpaste a solid. Day three, I was the real terrorist; and day four, the x-ray image of an elderly man of about eighty's bag, showed me that dildos come in all shapes and sizes and have no age limit. Rainforest prepare to be bulldozed and octopus pull out dem titties, it's-ink milking time.

I've got a lot to write.

# CHECKPOINT CHECKLIST

My airport has several terminals, each with three checkpoints for processing passengers. I generally only work in Terminal 1, cleverly titled in this way, primarily because of the societal establishment of chronological numerical sequence. Deviating from the system slightly, is Terminal 3. After asking a seventeen-year veteran of the company why Terminal 2 was missing, she had this to say: "I think there used to be a one and two but then they built three and tore down two." She paused to think, or just feign thinking, by rolling her eyes to the ceiling. She continued, "Come to think of it, two was gone before one was built so there was a two and three, but no one. Wait! That can't be right!" This went on long enough that at one point I forgot what I'd asked. The conversation played out like a one-man Abbott and Costello routine.

In each of the three checkpoints there are x-ray machines, a body scanner, metal detectors, and search stations; the number of machines depends on the passenger traffic through each. I've got a need, a need for speed, or in Lehman's terms, I'm an adult who either has ADD or the hyperactive thyroid of a squirrel on ecstasy. The best place to find action is the larger, busier checkpoints of Terminal 1. This is where you'll find me, strumming my pain with my fingers, singing my life with my words, killing me softly with my song, telling my whole life, with my werr-err-errr-ds.

Let's establish a few, important facts about me before you proceed. I am, I repeat, I am, a jackass. Just one who's actually a nice guy. A lot of my jackassery is used for public service; Larry Davidian. I wanna make people laugh. The best way to do that is by exposing my peculiar, teeny, deformed genitals. However, the police say it's not permitted in public, so as a compromise, I make jokes, tease, and make wildly inappropriate, confusing, stupid, wiener, comments. I'm lighthearted, care-free, easy-going, and a bunch of other words hyphenated together. I'm rolling around at an emotional state of two, only varying when hungover or if something I've just asked is repeated to me as a question.

I try to have fun in the checkpoint and at work in general, usually at others' expense. Surprisingly, my walk by, "I love you," and, "My butt hole really itches, can you get it for me?" comments are generally casually shrugged off by co-workers. I don't know exactly why this is. I assume they've determined me insane, believing only a lunatic would say what I'm saying, and are sympathetic to my mental illness. Either that or I must be horsing around; Kentucky Derby.

"Touch his balls. Do it! Do it!" I whisper into co-workers' ears as they prepare to pat-down elderly men with pacemakers. It doesn't even matter if I know the co-worker well. If not, even better. If the passenger overhears, another plus; I'm only strolling through, I won't be around for the awkward, questioning looks afterwards.

Sadly, but honestly, most of my inappropriate walk-by whispers are genital-related; low hanging fruit.

I digress.

# BIG PIMPIN

S creening officers at my airport bid for shifts twice a year to determine our schedule. The bidding is done by seniority, theoretically saturating to worse shifts as more people bid. With over two thousand employees, it's hard to move up the ranks. I sit pretty low on the totem-pole, maybe three-quarters of the way down. I'm full-time now; however, I remained a member of the part-time caste for nearly three years of employment. What's the advantage of full-time? Paid sick days. Some dental coverage? I guess. Although, to be honest, in the two years since I've been receiving benefits, I've avoided being mouth-molested by a stubby-fingered, dental diddler. Colgate seems to have me covered.

Luckily, my training group started half-way through a shift cycle and despite our poor seniority, were given nice midday shifts; eleven to three. I settled in well and made friends with a few employees who were roughly my age and working a similar shift. We started hanging.

It didn't take me long to commit the first cardinal sin of work: Don't date co-workers. It wasn't my first brush with the taboo workplace incest. I'd had a few hiccups while at the phone company. Okay, more than a few; but, hey, I worked the late shift and crap got boring. How do you liven up a quiet, four in the morning? Take your work girlfriend to the warehouse, set up a customer's repaired phone's video on record, and smash it out against the jog-ball storage shelf. Duh, everyone knows that. I never got in trouble for the tumultuous transgressions, but did have to sign off on a few unofficial vacations that closely resembled blackmail.

On a sunny, Wednesday afternoon, my friends and I finished our shift at the airport and met in Linda's backyard for a BBQ. I got drunk, as you do at these types of things. My car forgot to remind me he was there and so a co-worker who lived close to me offered up a ride. For that suggestion, I smashed her face in with a bottle. No, actually, I accepted. We got to my house and I asked, "Wanna go to the bar and watch me turn this buzz into obnoxious drunk?"

She laughed, and then answered, "Yeah, I need a drink. Let's park my car at mine then go to the bar."

*Fergie's meth hole echoed in the background, "OH SNAP. OH SNAP." We've got ourselves a gamer.

"You live closer, let's go to yours," Michelle offered. What a gentlewoman, she wanted to walk me home. My last attempt at push-ups left me lying on my stomach shaking and wheezing at thirteen-and-a half; I'd take the protection she provided through dimly lit streets.

She started kissing me as soon as we got inside. I don't know how I'd missed it. I was Alicia Silverstone's best movies, title. As a composer of 80's porn music who was missing his instruments would say, "Bow chica wow wow."

Cryptically, Michelle let me know that she didn't date co-workers. "I don't date co-workers," she stated, still laying on top of me, naked. "Shucks, too bad," I said. I thought, "Remember this for when you want to break things off and she's acting like your girlfriend."

The truth is, Michelle's non-commitment was imperative, I was waist deep in broads. EW! The day after the BBQ, I received a text from Linda saying her cousin, who'd been at the BBQ, thought I was attractive and wanted to go out. She was cute, chill, and not a drinker; but hey, that just meant more samples for me when we visited the liquor store together.

I texted, "Give her my number."

She came over later that week and we made the type of love you read about in Harlequin romance novels. Actually, it was pretty average, but just imagine if it was magical. None of this was a problem. The problem was to come.

An 11:00 a.m. to 3:00 p.m. and its extended version, 11 to 7, facilitated just the kind of lifestyle Gary, me, and my self-loathing, suicidal liver were accustomed to. Starting work early is great for ending work early and doing fun things in the evening. Starting work early is bad when you've been out late, got so drunk you thought a tree was your friend and chatted with it for a solid two minutes, only finishing the conversation because you noticed a cat bopping around nearby and decided to follow it to get an insight into its perspective on life. The conundrum is comparable to needing a girlfriend to get sex often, but having to have a girlfriend to do so.

Gary's Achilles heel is that he's a lush. On a full or empty stomach, he'll have two or three beers and be slurring his words, stopping mid-sentence to organize his brain and assess his surroundings. Picture someone who has recently woken from a three-year sleep. He made me feel more uncomfortable than sitting on a stool upside down. I constantly had to defend his drunkenness, do his talking for him, and order his next round or shot. Yes, I see why I shouldn't order him another drink, but I'm certainly not going to drink alone.

One night, Gary, Michelle, and I went to The Frog, our local. Forty-five minutes after leaving to take a piss, Gary still wasn't back. We decided he'd died so walked up to the bar to pay.

"What time are you off tonight?" I asked our waitress, Kendra.

"Twellll," she trailed off, simultaneously making that "Oh crap," face, and raising her arm to point to a wobbling Gary, inches from the floor-to-ceiling, front window of the bar. Gary, merely three drinks deep, was standing, swaying in the window, wacky-inflatable-flailing-balloon-man style. We watched as he dropped his phone, attempted to pick it up, dropped it again, fell, stood up, dropped it again and fell again, attempting to pick it up once more. Two minutes of this passed before he had it sturdily locked in his nose pickers. Elated, he swivelled, looking for a bystander to applaud his achievement. He rotated back to the window and caught eyes with us; his were unsteady. I put up my hand to request he wait one minute, but it was too late; he'd sprinted from the bar in what appeared to be, "Run for your life, Godzilla is coming," fear.

"Did you guys do a bunch of shots I didn't know about?" Kendra asked, concerned.

"Nope. I suspect Gary's just swapped out his liver with a three-year-old girl again."

She responded, "Explains why Simon said he saw him in the bathroom staring and talking to himself in the mirror for ten minutes, earlier. He said he was doing a B. Rabbit from 8 Mile rendition, shadow boxing the mirror at the same time."

"That had nothing to do with him being drunk and everything to do with him being prepared for our nightly rap battles."

She opened her mouth to ask if I was joking, but gave up. Instead, she chose to say, "Why do you think he ran away?"

Straight-faced, I answered, "Diarrhea. He poops his pants

a lot." Before she had a chance to ask if I was joking, Michelle and I walked away, leaving the question hanging in the air.

Speculating on Gary's thought process is a waste of time. Although, my guess is that he thought we were using kinetic powers to continually knock his phone out of his hand and ran away scared for however we would use the powers, next.

We started the ten-minute walk home and I saw a stray cat alluringly walking the streets; slutty feline. A light bulb went off in my head.

"Ima get him," I announced."

"You do you. I'll meet you at your place," Michelle responded. She'd only known me for a few months and already my delaying potential sex to run after a cat wasn't shocking to her. Aww, well. I chased the black and white evader for nearly an hour, finally capturing it in my arms. It's funny what drunk me is capable of. Sober, I find it exhausting to close a cupboard door. I carried the feline home and put it in a passed out Gary's room, before closing his door.

Because of our timetables that week, six days went by before I saw Gary again. Eventually, we crossed paths in our kitchen. I asked, "Dude, what the hell happened to you the other night? Were you on drugs?"

Perplexed, he replied, "Don't think so."

Equally perplexed, I asked, "Don't think so? No one's drugging you. You're a grown ass man who wore work boots to the bar. The only way anyone would drug you would be if they did it for a joke. Did you take drugs on your own?"

Again, he responded, "Don't think so."

I gave up.

The cat in his room wasn't mentioned once, then or after. I assume he ate it or somehow the cat morphed into him, turning him into a quarter cat, three-quarter human hybrid-human. I did notice him lapping milk out of a bowl more frequently, after the incident. Adding injury to stupidity, that same night he somehow lost his phone on the short walk, through brightly-lit roads.

My Casanova act drew a curtain call about a week after the car incident. Michelle called from my driveway to say she was coming in with coffees. I rolled over from my back, shifting to face ... Kendra, prepared to tell her the news.

WHA!!!!!!!

Time to follow the bouncing ball: hooked up with Michelle after the BBQ—hooked up with Linda's cousin a few days after that—continued to hook up with both—and now, here's the twist—was hooking up with Kendra, the server from my local bar, all the while. Before you get all bent out of shape, know this. Kendra knew about everyone, and everyone else knew everything was casual, therefore I'm not a jerk; I'm a stud muffin.

Surrendering, I said to Kendra, "Bar wench, I'm afraid things are about to become awkward. Michelle has just informed me she's coming in with coffees."

"It's Ms. Bar Wench to you, and hmmm. Now I make the tough decision of staying undressed while meeting your mistress or putting on clothes. Thoughts?"

"Let's compromise. Put on a costume."

Imagine catching a timid spider that had drank a growth potion and learned to speak, riffling through your nightstand, explaining to you why he was holding your condom in his mouth. That's about how the conversation between the three of us went.

I told you Linda's cousin doesn't drink, right? Yeah, so I had to end that. Around finishing my fourth pint in front of a non-drinker, I start thinking, "Go on Judgy McJudgerpants. Judge away."

David Copperfield has more trouble making women disappear.

Once again, afternoon drinking involved only Gary, me and that damned giant spider.

Our four months of late-night benders screeched to a halt when, due to low seniority, I landed a 6:00 a.m. to 10:00 a.m. shift in the next bid. Benders effortlessly slid to early afternoon. I soon learned the joys of 'Happy Hour', and how close to exploding an All You Can Eat, Indian lunch buffet could get me.

# TYPES OF PASSENGERS

W ithout looking up from my fixated, yet absentminded stare, I've ascertained what type of passenger you are. It may be the way your loose, cargo, zip-off pant/shorts look freshly plucked off the Poor Taste stores, First Time Travelling shelf; or that I first caught your entry movements nearly ten minutes ago, only to see those same motions repeated fifty-seven times, one for every sickening wave goodbye you gave to a loved one. Maybe, it's a noise: perhaps the sucking of teeth, illustrating a prick in my presence. Generally speaking, we know what kinda traveller you are, but do you?

Here's a bunch. See where you fit.

**First Time Traveller:**

This doesn't necessarily mean you're literally a first-time traveller. Attributes include: More questions than a six-year-old on an eight-hour road trip; a tentativeness reserved for visiting Michael Jackson's doctor; and clichéd remarks, (Examples: "I wonder what I forgot this time." "Do you know how far my gate is?")

### Captain Complainy Pants:

Enters the checkpoint and asks the boarding pass scanner, "Why is the lineup way over here?" After being told by the randomizer to go to his left, he asks, "Why can't I go to that line? It looks shorter." At the divest station he inevitably remarks, "We are still doing shoes, are we." A question turned into a statement—unnecessary and meaningless. On beeping, while walking through the metal detector, he states, "You need some consistency with these things. I'll beep here, but not in Moscow." His arms will shoot up when he sees his bag rejected, and then something like, "I always get flagged," will ejaculate from his ill-informed mouth. Finally, he'll guess what is being searched, none of which is correct. Upon completion, he'll part with, "You guys need to get some consistency."

### The Apologizer:

Psychologically, I'm sure there's a Freudian explanation for someone who apologizes for everything they do. I'm assuming it stems from getting caught by their mom at a young age masturbating ... about their mom. Unless you're going to say 'I'm sorry' like a grown man, acting like a grown man pretending to be a baby, who for some reason has a mock-sexy voice, then cut it out. Everyone should be entitled to one apology at the airport, and from my experience, you better save that for when you vomit on an employee's face, or your dog dry humps a handicapped child in a wheelchair.

### Gotta Be Babied Passenger:

They've got the eyes of a puppy and the torso of someone

who eats Kraft dinner like it's an Italian delicacy, extinct but to a few hundred boxes —in the trunk of their car. That's a knock-off of a Bob Saget joke; back to my joke.

Standing stalk-still, this passenger moves only when instructed, choosing to observe the screening officer out of the top of their eyes. Movements are delicate and tentative, a glass figurine molested at youth. Eventually, they may try things themselves, gingerly pulling a bin, careful to peek up every few seconds, making sure a rain of sharp reprimand isn't coming their way.

"Like this?" is their favourite question. Things like, "Is that it?" and, "Am I done?" are always asked. Softly delivered versions of every item in their bags is related, as their folded over frames gasp for relief.

On the other end of the line, the movements are repeated as they collect their bags then skitter away mouse-like, prepared to scat somewhere.

### All-in-One-Bin:

Have you ever seen how a child's ice-cream sundae turns out when you take them to a make-your-own-sundae place? Yeah, that's how these passengers' bins end up looking. Most walk up to the divest station; launch a heavy, thick bag upwards, and thump it into its intended target. They grab what's left of their belongings, cram those into the same bin, find some other crap lying around and rest that on top like the cherry. They make a magician's, "Tada," gesture with their hands, leaving them lingering close in case an avalanche of their junk begins cascading down their other junk, and voilà! They're set to go.

### Walk Through the Walk-through With All Your Bags:

A great man once said, "To get inside the mind of a crazy person, you yourself have to become crazy." That great man: me.

Basics of this passenger: They have their boarding pass scanned. Three feet away is the divest table. Ten feet away is the metal detector. In between, carpet. With a rolly bag – and this is very important because they always have a rolly bag - they walk past the divest station and towards the metal detector. There are two versions of this walk.

Version 1. Eyes focused straight ahead. Brisk, certain.

Version 2. Side-to-side head scanning aimed, for some unknown reason, at spots low to the ground. Like a lethargic pinball, these people manage to bounce off at least one item of security furniture, before eventually bashing the metal detector into full beep mode.

Screeners have a few methods of addressing these passengers. The main one is to become aggressive, shouting and hand motioning them to the divest station. A not so popular one, really only applied by my friend Adam and I, is to allow them to come all the way through, acting casual over their misjudgment. Once they've made it, and inevitably are staring heavenward for an answer to spastic alarm noises, we casually say, "Where you cowboys riding off to in such a hurry? You need to go back there and divest," or some such thing.

**Too Good For This:**

You know that face. The one Donald Trump makes anytime someone asks him a question he doesn't like and/or doesn't know the answer to. Facial expressions that are dead ringers for a bum hole, if a bum hole was a face. Every movement made by this passenger, in removing articles of clothing, is done aggressively. Laptops slammed into bins. Bins then pushed with the vigour of a playground bully. Sucking of the teeth, sighing and staring at the roof without moving their necks, are sure signs. Any mistake they've made stirs exasperation, as if their forgetting a cellphone in their jean's pockets is everyone else fault.

### "It's Medicinal":

You can see the smug look on this passenger's face, before you've even recited the liquid rule to them. They can barely hold the "It's medicinal" in, until you've finished the spiel. The veteran, 'It's medicinal', passenger usually doesn't flinch while delivering their line, indifferently spewing the words off-cuff. The rookies, who've been informed by friends, family, or are just privy from a fortunate overhear on a past flight, usually take a tentative stab—much like a child telling their first lie. You know that their first words to their travel-mates after leaving are, "That worked!! I can't believe it actually worked. I thought Elijah was pulling a prank on me when he told me I could just say - *COMPANY SECRET* -. Who could ever possibly drink these many juice-boxes in one flight?"

### Old Man Who Just Doesn't Care:

I've already considered how my old age will play out. The day I turn sixty, I'll toss out every garment I own that's un-comfortable. Jeans and dress pants—in the trash. Anything with buttons is gonzo. Despite an outfit representative of an athlete, I'll do no physical activities. That's where my twenty-year-old mail-order bride comes into play.

When an elderly passenger refuses to take off his shoes at airport security, I get it. I also respect it. My grandfather lived in a house next to a park. Kids cut across his front yard to get there quicker. In response, he put up a rope fence and a sign that said, 'Anyone caught trespassing, will be shot'. I believe he'd do it. The only things he enjoyed more than talking about which routes to take to get to places, was shooting things. That's my sample of what old age needs look like.

These geezers are over it. When they first flew, there was no such thing as airport security. You could smoke on planes. It was almost disrespectful not to slap a flight attendant's rump. So, they think, why should I remove my eight-gallon tin of mints from my pocket? What's going to keep my pants up if I remove my eighteen-pound belt buckle and suspenders? I see you, Old Man Who Just Doesn't Care, and I appreciate you.

### But, I Have TSA Pre:

Have you ever proclaimed, "But, I have TSA Pre-check,"? You're a prick. If an airport screening officer is addressing something you've done, an object even as exclusive as a membership that includes millions of other people, does not matter. TSA Pre is the equivalent of an airport Costco card. Enjoy your slightly shorter line, your ability to keep your shoes on if they don't alarm, and leave it at that.

### Are We Doing ... Today?:

The rules change ... oh, every 9/11 or so, so whyyyyyy, do certain passengers act as if the rules change daily? The passenger begins the question with a head-bob, similar to a chicken. Next, a raise of the forehead, slightly more predominate on one side. Then, spoken in overcompensating frat boy:, "We doing shoes today?" or, "We doing laptops?" The implication being yesterday they didn't. From my experience, they might not have yesterday, but not for lack of effort on my behalf. Actually ... yes, for lack of effort on my behalf, but not other screeners. You were definitely asked to take it out yesterday, but didn't. When your bag was rejected and the bag search screener asked, "Do you have a laptop in your bag?" you replied, "Ah, sorry. I didn't know we were doing laptops today."

### Overly Excited to Fly only to Find out he's Going Somewhere Crappy:

Every once in a while, an overly excited passenger sidles up to boarding pass scanner. They are jovial, oversharing, and busting a nut to get on a plane. Most of the time, this engrosses the screening officer as well, temporarily immersing them in the collective joy. That's until, you scan the pass and *Dead Snake*

*Lake*, *Nebraska* pops up on the monitor. Now you actually take in the passenger. Notice that the sleeve monster, never travelling too far from trailer parks, has devoured the arms of his blouse. The tooth fairy got a bit overzealous in his tobacco chew vault. If it wasn't for the mud, oil, and what may be blood smeared over them, a pair of jeans holier than Southern Baptist ministers would be staring up at you. I guess, you can take the redneck outta the trailer, but you can't stop the redneck from getting excited to get home to his sister/cousin/wife for some nookie and squirrel stew.

### Over-Sharer:

Prime example: I was doing bag search and received a small suitcase, marked because it contained an area dense with metal. I identified the owner, a birdie lady of about fifty. *Side note: Over sharers are almost always bird-like ladies of about fifty. They are nearly always frail, poorly-dressed in pastels, covered in kittens; smell like cigarette smoke, have bad teeth, make the movements of a lizard's head and their overall presence screams, I have a La-Z-Boy chair on my porch and a broken-down car in my backyard. This passenger was no exception.

"Ma'am, I just need to have a look in your bag. I think it's just change."

So it began.

"I'm so sorry. I was just here for a funeral and I don't know why I brought it. I was staying with my sister in Ithaca and we'd just gone out for lunch to Denny's, the one on I-97, we had this really sweet server, Susie, I think her name was."

I interrupted.

I screamed, "No one cares lady," while shaking the piss outta her. Naw, just playing. I said, "That's okay. I'm just going to check inside your bag, quickly. Change is fine."

As I sifted through the pennies (yes, all of it was pennies) she recounted her weekend in minuscule detail. I finished the search and told her, "I'm all done. You can take the bag. Have a nice day."

She, however, was not done.

"I don't even know why I brought all those pennies. I mean, I was in such a rush getting to the funeral. I barely had time to pack. Do you know how much flights cost last minute?"

That kept going on for soooo long and for dramatic effect I'd keep writing it out, if I wasn't afraid to run out of computer keyboard ink.

Finally, she finished with, "Anyways, do you want them?"

Straight-faced and without flinching, I responded, "No."

She wasn't to be deterred, nor was she going to shut up anytime soon.

She asked, "Well what should I do with them?"

I took a deep breath, repressing an urge to say, "Shove them in your mouth so you can't talk."

I answered, "Find a wishing well."

Giddy, she asked, "Do you know where I can find one?"

She really said that. Is sarcasm taught in Ithaca? In lizard cages?

"No," I began. "If I did, we wouldn't be having this conversation."

Now, she could have taken the comment in a multiple number of ways. The more pleasant of them being that I was implying I'd have used my wishes to be rich, secure in a castle, in my bedroom, in a bed, covered in prostitutes, far from her. What I meant was that I'd have wished her away, or never to have come in the first place—and she knew that—and unlike fashion sense, she got it. She left, mumbling about how she'd get from the airport to her aquarium.

**Want To Be Touched:**

Cougars and horny old dudes, I'm looking at you. Yep,

they make up about ninety-five percent of the passengers who suggest someone of the opposite sex pat them down. Every once in a while you get a passenger, like my buddy James did the other day, an ex-prison guard who upon alarming at the metal detector, placed his hands on the x-ray machine, spread his legs, leaned forward and said, "Go ahead, do the cavity search. I use to work in the prison system and I know the drill."

Usually though, it's just a lady of about fifty-five wearing a loose, flowing, leopard-print blouse, returning from a one week all-inclusive trip to Belize, who alarms and instantly says, "I'm okay if a man does it," then winks or deviously smiles. Lady, I've seen porn too, get over yourself. Lucky for these females, their proposition is always, always less creepy than when an older man does it.

### My Shoes Too?

You ma'am/sir know who you are. You look at everyone else removing their shoes, squint, then ask, "My shoes too?" You damn well know, your shoes too. Do not say, "What if I didn't re-member socks?" Because that opens up a wholeeeeeeee new bag of worms.

### Pre-emptive Asker:

You're quick —I'll give it to you. You spit questions out right before a screener can deliver instructions, each one delay-ing them just enough that you can squeak in another millisec-onds ahead of theirs; but wait. Who said, 'Patients is a virtue'? Was it a grammatically inept, business proficient doctor? So eat your words, pre-emptive asker. Give it a second. There's no rush. It's not like you have a plane to catch or something.

### The Inappropriate Asker:

I've been asked, "You guys hiring?" by a guy, standing next to me, at a urinal, as if somehow cock peripheral doubles as a resume. At Subway, still four people back from choosing my toppings, a suited-man, clean in appearance, and dirty in mind, said to me, "Must be nice seeing all those tits in the full body scanner." Clearly high, another passenger once grabbed hold of my shirt as I walked the halls during break. Sincerely, he asked, "Where are the confiscated drugs stored? We could go halves." I thought, 'If there were stored drugs and I knew where they were, I wouldn't be standing here, pal.'

### Chirp Artist:

Do you linger behind a friend whose bag is being checked, chiming in with an unproductive, "Ohhh, Gary. What did you forget this time? Is this your first time travelling, or what?"? You sir, are a chirp artist.

### Look at My Belly:

There is a group of passengers, generally of the same two ethnicity's and male, who lift their shirts up, roughly around nipple, over almost any inquiry by airport security. I don't want to fuel stereotypes, although for illustration purposes I must divulge the main culprits—at least with a subtle hint. One group, let's call them, *Delicate Plate Males*, can be found chopping boards in half with their hands. For North American children to visit them, a technique of digging a deep, deep hole in their backyard is often applied. Be careful of the earth's molten core.

The other group of people became famous when an urchin from a ghetto in their country was able to win a television trivia game, leaving his pockets bursting with Rupees.

Let me get right inside the mind of these voyeurs for this one.

I walk up to the divest station holding my bags, I've just had some butter chicken for lunch and I'm feeling gassy; still, excited to fly. I place one bag in a bin, another on top of that, and yet another on that one. I've made a pretty great tower, if I do say so myself. A militantly-dressed female moves my belongings around, adjusting them into what I've heard others refer to as organized. I don't care that she's jostling my luggage though, because they all have broken zippers, making them nearly impossible for anyone, including myself to open. The ones that do have a zipper are locked, and I have no idea where the key is. I pretend to look at her for instructions, however, the jokes on her, I'm farting and only have my eyes open because eyes-closed, grownup farting is weird.

She aggressively pats her pockets. I wobble my head. She does it again. I do it again. She's discernibly upset. I wobble my head. She gestures at her belt. I lift my shirt over my belly. "That's it there love, my glorious butter chicken vault. Get a look at this cauldron of love. Have you ever seen anything sexier? You wanna rub it?" She throws her arms up in surrender and I take the opportunity to squeeze in a head wobble. She shews me away.

Who's next in line to see my belly? I may as well leave my shirt up to save some time. I walk towards an opening; that's not for me. A barrier with bright red crosses through illustrations seems more inviting and I ram into that, demonstrating my good ramming skills. Two frantic, militantly-dressed people put their arms up and wave, I'm assuming to encourage more ramming. I ram away. Eventually, ramming becomes tiring and I move to the opening. I make that slender box my bitch, bouncing off it with flair. Popping out the other side, I lift my arms and show everyone my airplane pose, holding it while head-wobbling for good measure.

The male starts running a black stick over my body, pausing every couple inches, always indicating for me to materialize the hidden treasures stored in each nook and cranny of my heavy garb. Thirteen hours later we are done. Both employees are lying face down on the ground drenched in sweat. I fart.

Where's my bag? I can't find it. I stop looking directly in front of me and sit down. Thirty minutes later someone tugs on my sleeve, pointing to a bag covered with a piece of paper with writing on it. For some reason, the words on the paper have my name and address, but that can't be my bag, no. I better go back to sitting down. Twenty minutes later, I think, 'Ya know what, perhaps that is my bag'. Then I fart. I walk over to the bag and blankly stare at a person moving their mouth while struggling to unzip it. I attempt to leave, hoping to return to sitting and farting, but am called back. Someone has a bad case of the impatience.

To my surprise, a pedestrian explains to me in my second language that eighteen jars of peanut butter and fifty jars of Vaseline are not allowed. I'm given options and pretend I'm going to call someone to retrieve them. Jokes on them though, I don't have any numbers, and even if I did, my phone doesn't work, it's in eight pieces in a security bin somewhere unknown to me. I flick my wrist dismissively. A lady pushing a wheelchair arrives behind me and, in baby-talk, asks if I'd like to sit down. I was born in America and resent the condescension. "Ma'am," I begin. "Let's get going. I've got a flight to catch." I sprint over to the chair and hop in, allowing the friction with seat rubber to mask my fart noise. Two hours to get through airport security: my new record.

**Cliché:**

When travelling through airport security, do you say any of the following?

After entering an empty checkpoint:
"I've never seen it so dead in here."
"I should always travel at this time."

On getting 4s on a boarding pass:
"I should play the lottery."
"Guess it's my lucky day."

On a bag being sent for search:

"I always get flagged."

"I fly all the time and I never get stopped. I don't know what it could be."

"My bag's over there. What should I do?"

On the rules:

"You guys need to have more consistency."

"The rules are different everywhere."

"Are we doing shoes today?"

"You guys still doing shoes?"

"Soon you'll be making us get naked."

### Missed Geology in School Passenger:

This gem happened to my friend Mohamed, at work: A passenger walked through the metal detector and it alarmed. He was sent back and told to remove any metal from his person. When he walked through a second time it alarmed again. Mo scanned him, pausing at his front pocket to resolve an alarm. "What have you got in here?" he asked. The passenger pulled out an iPhone. Mo assumed the man would see his mistake and apologize or give an, 'Ohhh'. He didn't. Mo said, "It's your phone that's alarming, it's made of metal." The passenger, flabbergasted, responded, "Not this one. I got the waterproof version so it wouldn't alarm." Mo exploded from stimuli overload, his brains cling to the airport ceiling to this day.

Honestly, this type of interaction isn't that uncommon at the metal detector.

### Know What Alarmed:

Little Guessy Guessorsons, just guessing away at everything. Save your breath, and your guesses, we know why you alarmed, or, almost always have a better idea than you. If I hear,

"It's my zipper," one more time ... that'll be one more time than I'd heard it total—previous to hearing it that time. If, it's "My buckles. They always alarm," then take off your ever alarming buckles before coming through and save us both some time. If it's, "Oops, I forgot my change. That's what it is," then don't forget your change, place it in a gosh-darn bin with the rest of your crap. Knowing what alarmed doesn't make you prophetic: it makes you forgetful or lazy.

### The Know it, But Don't Show it:

There's a certain type of passenger, let's call them Nexus/Pre to make it easy, who brush away help as soon as it is offered by screening officers. The implication is that they've done it a million times, they know what's up. Well, guess f-ing what, Nexus/Pre, y'all are alarming just as much as everybody else. How about while you're taking that stick out of your ass, you reach up a few feet further after and remove your BlackBerry from your pocket; and don't even get me started on laptops ... grrr.

### The Repeat Offender Repeat Offender:

There's a sick joke being played by passengers these days. One I'm sure has been orchestrated by some deranged, twisted prankster. In a common scene illustrating this joke, four passengers line up to divest. To save time and my voice, I make one large announcement, "Everybody take out their large electronics, remove your shoes, remove your jackets, and take any metal out of your pocket."

Sorted.

What could go misinterpreted?

Divest station 1: "Should I take my shoes off?"
Me: "Yes."
Divest station 1: "So, yes to shoes?"

Me: "Yes."

Divest station 3: "Laptop?"

Me: "Yes."

Divest station 3: "Even mine?"

Me: *Angry stare.

Divest station 1: "Did you say yes to shoes?"

Me: *Angry stare.

Divest station 4: "Sir, do you guys need iPads out?"

Me: "Laptops."

Divest station 4: "So no iPad?"

Me: *Angry stare.

Divest station 1: "Sorry, I didn't hear you. Are we?"

Me: *Angry stare.

Divest station 2: *Looks at everybody taking off shoes. "Are we doing shoes?"

Me: *Internally cocks a gun.

Divest station 3: "Is a tablet a laptop?"

Me: *Mumbles under breath, "I'm going to bash you to death with a tablet."

Divest station 3: "So no? Leave it in?"

Divest station 1: "Phone?"

Divest station 4: "Should I take off my jacket?"

### 21 Questions Guy:

"Sir, please remove your laptop and large electronics and take off your shoes."

"Laptop?"

"Yes."

"Anything else? Phone?"

"Large electronics."

"Does my Nintendo Switch count?"

"As what?"

"A large electronic?"

"No."

"Okay. What about my phone?"

"Anything the size of a laptop or larger."

"Gottcha. So, I can bring my phone?"

"Bring it where?"

"With me."

"You mean in your pockets through the metal detector?"

"Yeah."

"No."

"Okay." *Puts phone into pocket. "What about my wallet?"

"What about it?"

"Is it metal?"

"Why are you asking me? Is it?"

"I don't think so. I'll just leave it in the bin." *Puts it in his pocket.        "What about my chain?"

"What about it?"

"Should I take it off?"

"No."

*Thinks hard. Runs it through his hands. Looks heavenwards. Leaves it on.

"We doing shoes?"

"I already addressed that."

"So?"

"So, yes."

"Okay. Anything else?"

"Please leave."

**Event passenger:**

Periodically, someone sweeps through the airport and leaves behind an epic wake. Something airport employees and often the general public are left re-telling for years. In conversation with co-workers, the episode is usually referred to more or less the same way. Person A begins with, "Remember that guy who ran through the metal detector naked?" Then Person B responds with something like, "Oh yeah, that guy. I almost forgot about that."

These are people you don't want to be. To avoid becoming such a passenger, adhere to my following advice.

- Empty your bladder before you enter a security checkpoint.
- Take your meds.
- Remember what normal people behave like, and then follow that example.
- If you're confused, ask questions first, act second.
- Keep your hog put away.
- Leave your dead animals at home.

**The Business Man/Wombman:**

All business, man. Few words. More streamlined than Venice.

# SOP

I mentioned SOP earlier, without an explanation. My bad. Essentially, they are Big Brother's guidelines for how and what airport screening officers should do at work. SOP, like in most industries, stands for standard operating procedure. The one exception I can think of for the acronym is in the stripper business. There, it obviously stands for, sucking off policy. Patrons suffering from dentophobia, appreciate clubs that follow these conditions strictly.

In airport security, this is supposed to be our bible – and how appropriate that Big Brother created it—seeing as they treat themselves as if they're all-knowing perfect deities. Almost every small detail is listed, including what day neckties can be removed for the summer season. What kinda fecal-nuts, fairy-tale world do these dinks live in that temperatures adjust seasonally on exact days? Would it be so hard for them to give us some discretion on ties? Like, it's a hundred and five out, but the SOP says you can't remove them until tomorrow, and don't even think about getting heat stroke, the SOP firmly states no heat stroke while in the checkpoint. Another thing, our uniforms have many renditions: vest; long-sleeved sweaters; T-shirts; long shirt; pants; skirts. Okay, I guess not that many—but enough that your average passenger isn't lulled into compliance by coordination. If you asked them after their checkpoint experience, whether the guy taking their dead grandma's jam from them wore a tie or not, I'm thinking they wouldn't know or care. It makes you wonder what high-up in the tie industry had dirt on the SOP committee when they were drawing up the specs.

CEO of SOP, Bill, stands around a large table of well-dressed, official-looking peeps: "Well guys, I think March would be a perfectly acceptable month to remove ties. Weather can sometimes take a turn for the warm."

Laughter.

Evil corporate lawyer-looking chap squints his eyes and stares darts into Bill.

Bill hesitantly corrects himself: "April."

Pan into evil lawyer, now squinting harder.

Bill is now sweating, terrified. "May?"

Slow head shake.

"June."

Evil corporate lawyer sits back content; Big tie wins again.

Departing from its seemingly strict, unbending format, there are also things missing from the SOP, and others items are only vaguely explained. Of course, this presents a lot of problems. For one, anything that isn't listed is open to interpretation. This wouldn't necessarily be the worst thing, if you hired normal-thinking, reasonable people. This isn't the case for airport security. If there was one, our HR's SOP for hiring people would probably look something like this:

Only hire people, who adhere to the following criteria:

- Temperament: Short.
- Aliens: People who can respond to interview questions about aliens.

HR problems aside, the SOP needs to change sometimes, in order to address new problems or technology. These adjustments are rarely communicated immediately or to all of the employees. I think they exist on some Big Brother database, but as if I remember my login. If it wasn't for Auto-save, I wouldn't have access to any one of the social media accounts I access daily. Give me a break with password retrieval questions. Who was my best friend in grade eight? My guess is whichever one had access to their father's porn mag collection, at the time I made my account. Realistically, whoever had the best toy collection or hottest mom.

Needless to say, you don't want to be the guy who rolls into work rocking a George Hamilton tan, feeling all loosey goosey, after a week's vacay in Cuba and catch a grenade slide by on the x-ray screen, panic, hit the alarm, flee the building screaming hysterically like a dumped banshee, only to be informed that the rules changed while you were away—grenades are now allowed on planes.

I ain't keeping up with SOP changes. My co-workers ain't. Hell, management is equally clueless.

A typical conversation between employees when confronted by an SOP dilemma, plays out like arguments I had with friends when I was a kid, pre-Google and where the final word was always, "If you don't believe me, ask my mom." Take this conversation I had with a passenger for example:

Me: "Sir, I'm not sure if skates are allowed. Just give me a second to double-check."

Passenger: "You shouldn't need to check, you should know your job."

Me: "Well, I don't. I hardly know anything related to this job."

Passenger: "Well you should."

I settled in. I love a game of well-you-should, well-I-don't.

Me in a childish, nasally hum: "Unnnnn-uhhhh."

I waited for a, "Uhhhh-haaa," but it never came.

Passenger: "What's the point of you being here if you don't know your job?"

Me: "Money. Duh. Do you think doctors know every medicine? Disease?"

Passenger: "You're not a doctor."

I laughed, and said, "Am too. I'm going to be your proctologist soon enough."

He sighed and stood still. I followed suit. He cracked first.

Passenger: "Can you please go check? I've got a flight to catch and you not knowing your job is going to make me miss it." He mumbled a bunch of swears under his breath.

Me: "Sorry, I was digging through my memory, searching to see if I knew the answer to this whole skate conundrum somewhere deep inside me."

Passenger, sharply: "Well hurry."

I turned to a co-worker checking a bag next to me.

Me: "Hey Brad, do you know if skates are allowed?"

Brad: "Crap, not sure. I usually just say no to anything I'm not sure about."

Me: "I think they are."

Another co-worker came over to weigh in.

Tim: "I think they are allowed if the blades can't be removed."

Me: "But with the right tool I'm sure the blade can always come off."

Brad: "Good point."

Passenger: "Are you guys serious right now? None of you idiots know how to do your job? I've got a plane to catch. How long is this going to take?"

Now, here's the thing with being a dick to airport security. We may not be able to arrest you, or really do anything with authority, however, what we can do is take sooooo long that you *will* either miss your plane, do something in anger that we *can* have you arrested for, or give-up and agree to leave your precious belongings behind. All three of us went into that mode.

It was time for the supervisor to play the role of mom.

"Yo, Doug, skates allowed?"

Supervisor Doug: "I'm not sure. Let me check online."

Five minutes later.

Doug: "The internet isn't working. I'll call someone."

Passenger: *Deep sigh. Aggressive eye-roll and exasperated body-language.

Me: "So, what you boys doing this weekend?"

Brad: "Getting soooo drunk."

Passenger: *Looks at blade; looks at watch; looks at our throats. "Guys? Seriously? I've got a plane to catch. Hurry up?"

The three of us collectively create a shield, blocking the passenger.

Supervisor Doug returns seven minutes later and says, "Okay, they're allowed."

Me, one second later: "Sorry Sir, our boss just informed us that they aren't allowed."

Passenger: "I just heard him say they were."

Me: "Psych."

I indifferently handed him the skates and began turning

back to Brad and Tim. In the midst of my perfect-ten pirouette, I heard my pet peeve: under the breath swears.

"Stupid assholes," he whispered.

Grow some balls man. In most cases, swears don't get you thrown in the slammer, or a lake, only maybe into a wall if your jaded swear victim is sensitive and violent. Personally, at work, I want passengers to free themselves from the burdensome pussyness that seems to be plaguing the vast majority. You swear, I swear, we all swear for ice-cream, but swearing under your breath? That's childish. Undermining. So, I did what I had to do.

"Sir," I shouted to gain his attention. About five feet away, he stopped and turned back, taking a few steps nearer. I leaned across my work station, getting as close as possible.

I slowly articulated words, that in print would be bold letters, like this, "YOU ARE A STUPID ASSHOLE," then pretended to mic-drop.

The passenger horse-sneezed then sped walked away. Assuming an enthusiastic response from my co-workers, I spun to them with a smile. Neither was paying attention, both brushing the event off as another one of my typical altercations, before seeing my decisive knock-out blow.

What's worse than our ignorance over the SOP is the passengers' knowledge of it. Somehow, a particular group of passengers seems to have no problem learning and reciting the SOP to us daily. Where are they learning this crap? Does some diligent screener have a twitter account with millions of followers that he updates with SOP changes?

Screenerguy67:

Good news ladies and gentlemen, we've (airport security) reinstated nail files on the permitted items list. No more uneven edges :) January 13$^{th, 2019}$

Either way, they know the required size of liquids and

knives to the centimetre and millilitre. They know when we can and cannot just shove them inside the body scanner, instead of patting them down; and—my all-time favourite—they know what counts as medicinal in regards to otherwise prohibited items.

"Sir, this is over the liquids, gels and aerosol limit of 3 oz," my partner and friend, May, recited to an older man of about sixty-five. He looked sprig, stuffed with zeal and spunk; the kinda guy you'd catch at Fat Tuesday's drunk on old fashions at eleven on a Thursday night. The oversized gel was KY jelly. For those unfamiliar with dick performance enhancers; spermicidal lube. Without hesitation, embarrassment, or breaking eye-contact, Big Swinging Dick Danny explained, "It's medicinal."

I'd seen the lube from my spot a few feet away and expected a usual, timid, "Just throw it away. I forgot it was in there." Not some confident stud standing on a rooftop, shouting to the masses, "Yes, this is my penis gel. Yes, I use it; often!!!"

I listened in.

"Okay," May responded. The process is to swab medicinal items, then let them go. As she did this, Danny shocked us even further.

"I use it for my catheter," he volunteered.

Usually, I'd think talking about an item you shove into your privates, with someone who's holding said item, would be kinda gross and weird. Not with Big Swinging Dick Danny. I got the impression there is some sex thing out there I don't know about—something involving KY, catheters and older people getting cray cray in a bad way.

In the testing process, Danny solidified my suspicions. Still standing up straight, and with projection that demonstrated he thought it needed to be heard, he added, "What did you think it was for, a good time?" before winking.

May sped through the process and quickly packed his bag

back up, finishing with, "Thank you. Everything is fine. Thank you," then turning to me for moral support. The man left, probably to bang a flight attendant or pilot in some adventuresome way that I don't even know about.

Needless to say; when I travel, it's with gallon-size tubs of medicinal margaritas, mudslides, and G&Ts. I suggest you do the same. Just say your doctor prescribed them for your nerves, thick blood, and hatred for looking at unattractive people; I've got ya.

# MENTAL WITH METAL

I assume that most, if not every adult took geology in school. At the very least, parents or a friend explained the consistency of different materials to them. You'd be hard-pressed to escape childhood without a bit of earthy, stony knowledge in the cranium. After all, it's essential to one's survival— when young and looking to make people laugh by getting whacked in the nuts with an object—to know whether it's a soft, gonad-friendly Nerf bat or a scrotal-crushing metal one. One will hurt, but you can probably walk it off; plus you'll have a ton more friends after the smack. The other leaves your genitals compressed into a diamond and people will think you're a dummy after the smack. If you work a day at the airport, you'll assume there are a lot of passengers walking around with precious stones in place of testicles. These people never figured out what metal is.

Roughly, ten percent of passengers whom I tell to place their cellphone in the tray, ask me, "Why?" This comment is after I tell them everything metal in their pockets needs to go into a bin. Even after I respond, "Because it's made of metal," they give me that squint-eyed, skeptical look that says, "I don't think so." Most people leave it at a look, not wanting to risk a debate on periodic table elements. My stern face and confidence in metal usually dissuade them to succumb.

Others argue, and this is where I become concerned for the world. The comment, "But my bracelet's silver, not metal," may as well be, "but it's water; why am I getting wet?" Or to me, it may as well be, "But I'm a big dumb idiot who literally knows nothing. Now please leave me alone so I can get on a big metal bird that is going to fly me to my vacation on the island, Russia."

In five years on the job, I've been told that phones, tablets, gold, silver, metal belt buckles, steel-toed boots, and metal/titanium body part replacements are not metal. One of the more absurd questions I've heard had to be, "How is my metal knee-brace setting off the metal detector?" Well, first off, genius, the answer is right there in your own question. He at least had the decency to register his ignorance after I explained. He continued with, "Wow I'm dumb." I couldn't stop my head and neck from involuntarily aggressively agreeing in a nod, as he walked back to remove it.

A lot of people assume things when they hear the beep-beep of the metal detector. "It's my zipper, isn't it?" is frequently asked. "It's my ring; it always goes off," and, "I have piercings," are both common. I'll give these people credit, both are commonly made of metal, just too small an amount to trigger the alarm. Maybe Beyoncé has rings so big and pure they set off a metal detector, but then again she's rich and charters, she'd never be flying with us peasants and needing to walk through security. She just arrives in a limo and hops on her giant metal bird.

Even worse than the things people don't think are metal, are the things that they do. Working S2, aka front, aka boring as, aka boarding pass scanner position, a few days into my first week after training, a middle-aged, female passenger came to a halt before me. At first glance, I thought a large bird had escaped wherever birds lived, dressed up in fancy clothes and decided to fly on a plane, saving herself the energy of flapping her wings. I took in her beaked nose, her feathery eyebrows and hair, and the shawl covering her wings. I asked, "Boarding pass please?" She handed it to me. She had hands. Perplexing. I gave her the rundown, sent her towards the metal detector, and then turned to chat with a friend. A second later, she was back, laughing. I asked, "What happened? Did you alarm?"

"Yes," she responded, "my scarf set it off." I looked at her scarf, it was grey but contained no metal-sequin or medallions.

"I don't think so," I replied. "You don't have a belt or jewellery on? Something in your pockets?"

"No dear," she said, giving me the 'you poor, stupid soul', look. "I told you, it's my scarf. See?" she said, offering it to me.

"It's silver, that's why it went off."

Her logic was, that because silver is metal, and metal sets off the metal detector, and her scarf was the colour silver, it set off the alarm.

"You're absolutely right," I muttered through lips held tight to avoid bursting out in laughter. I thought, "At least she knows silver is metal. That's more than I can say for a lot of passengers."

Not even a week in and I was already jaded by the idiots.

# I WANNA BE ...
# DRUNK FOR THIS

One of the most frequently asked questions by passengers, after having their alcohol confiscated, is about what is done with it. In five years, I've never officially been told. The rumour is firemen (or firewomen; after all, what female wouldn't want to slide down poles, hang around with hunky firemen, save cats and nap all day?) pick it up from a more-or-less hidden room, and then dump it out somewhere. This is where I should fill the page with HA HA HA HA HAs, but I'll save your eyes taking in too many H's and A's; it can wear out your irises.

But seriously, HA HA HAH!!!! Let's get real here for a second. Firefighters? The airport has police. They aren't qualified to dump it out? We even have adults, employed by the airport, who, to me at least, also seem pretty qualified to dump a liquid into something; even something with a small opening, I bet. I have a few firefighter buddies. They all have great home bars. Just saying—coincidence?

I'm not a scientist so I'm not going to pretend I know whether this whole hoopla is alcohol-spontaneously-starting-fire related. I do know, that same alcohol we're taking away, was almost always just on a plane. Is our airspace more flammable than other countries? Lighters are allowed on that same plane; and, for the ambitious pyro, sticks, i.e. kindling. I have to deduce then, there's no worry alcohol can create a fire on a plane. I've seen absinth come through, so I'm obviously not convinced at all, but let's not get into that. So, if it's safe on a plane, why can't it be safe in our garbage cans, or for us—seemingly adults—to dump somewhere. You ever wondered where firefighters get the bravery to walk into burning houses? Mmhm, you see what I'm getting at ... LOADEDDDD!!

Now, as I mentioned, I'm not a scientist; however, I am a keen observer. What I know is that it takes far less time to test a liquid than argue that someone's five hundred dollar bottle of scotch can't stay in their carry-on because it was bought an hour before the time requirement on its receipt. Everyone should already know that scotch turns explosive twenty-four hours and a minute after bought.

Whenever a passenger brings alcohol into our checkpoint, there are a few things we check for; that:

- It's in a duty-free bag;
- The bag is sealed;
- They have a current receipt;
- There's been no tampering

If all the criteria are met, then it's tested. If it passes, we reseal the bag and the passenger is free to bring it on their next flight. This process is not usually a problem. People get to keep their alcohol, therefore they are happy. The testing can be a bit slow (mostly because every employee hates doing it and takes their sweet time doing so) and sometimes this upsets the passenger. Although, for the most part they are patient.

Where a problem does arise, is when their duty-free doesn't fulfill one of the criteria. The reader may ask, "But if you have a machine that tests the alcohol to determine whether it's safe or not, why not just use that on every type of alcohol? Heck, let's get crazy here and ask, why not test every liquid that comes through? Then I won't have to throw away the jam I got in my grandma's will. The last jar she ever made, in fact."

Time??? I don't know!! I think that's the reason. Surprisingly, passengers don't ask that question. I sure do ask though. Have I ever got a response? HA HA HA. No, no, much like any other logical question I've ever asked management regarding our procedures.

Whoever decided on the protocol not to allow liquids meeting these guidelines, has never argued with a passenger about it. It would have saved me hours, actually hundreds of hours of time, if every liquid could just be tested. Again, I think the idea is that there *are* bad liquids out there, ones that can either be turned into explosives or already are explosive. Then again, we have machines to test whether they are, two-hundred-and-fifty-thousand dollar machines. The protocol for liquids that aren't alcohol, when confiscated, is to throw them in the trash. Why are we afraid of them going on the plane but not sitting next to employees in a garbage can?

Next, a cute little lady takes that garbage away and throws it in a dumpster. Why are we not afraid for that little lady, who's jostling around a bag filled with what we determined were possibly dangerous materials? Where is the logic? Where is the humanity? I could honestly go on about this forever. It may be the most infuriating airport security topic in my mind.

Not long after I started, liquid bottle bedlam begat me. The x-ray operator sent me a bag to search, pointing out what was obviously a bottle of booze. I waited for a few minutes before an elderly man, straight out of a Dostoevsky novel, stumbled up.

"Sir," I announced. "I'm going to be searching your bag.

Do you have any sharp or breakable objects in here?" (I've since done away with such formal interactions, substituting them with, "Your bag?" and nodding then reaching in blindly. However, at the time, I was new, fresh, and naive.)

Fyodor mumbled incomprehensibly in an Eastern European accent.

I asked, "Sooooo; no, or?"

More mumbles.

"Great."

I reached into the bag and grabbed a bottle of vodka, three-quarters gone. It didn't take a gut biologist to figure out where the rest was. The great Russian novelist stood stock-still, unperturbed by my finding.

"So," I began. "Any liquid over three ounces is not allowed in your carry-ohhhh, you can't do that!!" He'd snatched the bottle mid-way through my speech and started chugging. I hadn't been trained for this. I doubt even bartenders know how to react in these situations. I watched, mesmerized as he crushed it; finishing with the thirst-quenching relieved sigh of a glasses-wearing kid in a Coca-Cola commercial.

"Well, that's that," I stated, defeated, my body deflating in turn.

He wasn't done though. Apparently, the bottle and him weren't mates. He spiked the bottle like a famous volleyball player, if there was such a thing as a famous volleyball player. The shatter rang out through the checkpoint, earning everyone's attention.

"Clean up in aisle seven," I muttered, unsure what the hell else to do or say.

I noticed he was still peering down at the bottle, nearly a full minute after his assault, suggesting either a sorrowful resentment or a victor's stare down. It didn't really matter; the man was a maniac.

The x-ray operator edged behind me, using me as a shield from the cenosillicaphobia.

"You going to call the cops?" he asked.

I replied, "Naw, I can't be assed."

"What you going to do then?"

"Allow him to walk away, hope the supervisor didn't hear or see any of this, tell him I have diarrhea, and hope that I'm long gone before any of this needs to be dealt with."

"Aren't you new though?"

"Not new in the world buddy," I softly delivered as I sympathetically patted him on the back. Next, I got my doody break, trounced down some steps, made my way around a corner out of sight and pulled a tattered copy of Crime and Punishment from my cargo pockets; I needed to occupy my mind with words so my conscience didn't get the better of me.

# AIRPORT SHUTTLE

A few months into the morning shift, I started having trouble with my car. I don't know a lot about cars, other than their capacity for dead human trunk storage, so bear with me. My catalytic seismonigor backfired? Whatever, some crap backfired, regularly stopping my Passat in impractical locations. Because of this, I asked a couple different co-workers who lived nearby to be on a sort of standby for if/when my car had problems, before or after work. The problem required me to wake up even earlier than normal to start the engine and ascertain whether I'd need a lift, equalling more tinnitus, worse terrorism stopping, and an overall more easily agitated me.

The blood-curdling ding of my phone alarm woke me on Monday morning. Is there a pleasant phone alarm? How much wouldn't I give (probably not a lot, actually, but humour me) to live before electricity and alarm clocks.

"Don't think so, Betsy. Can't be before six, I haven't heard the roosters alarm us once."

"I heard them an hour ago. You need to get up and sow the oats."

"That was Bob's rooster darling. I've told you, he sets his for earlier than ours. Now get back to bed."

I slapped at my nightstand, knocking over my lamp (maybe should have turned that on before slapping around) nudged a glass of water, and finally felt the phone. Poking the snooze button, I instantly fell back asleep.

*Repeat above two more times.

I stumbled to the bathroom, deliberately avoided flicking on the lights until my tinnitus subsided; risking stubbed toes and bashed knees in the process. Putting toothbrush to jibs, I realized the toothpaste was still hanging out in the tube, laughing at my idiocy. Squeezing extra hard in retaliation, I thought, "How in all that's holy does my mouth hole smell like actual crap every morning when the last thing I've put in it was toothpaste?"

I threw on the same work clothes I'd worn the day before, went to the kitchen to pack my lunch, then made my way from my apartment to the driveway, where some complete dink had dumped two feet of snow and minus twenty degrees of hell. I turned the key over in the ignition; neither optimistic nor awake enough to be considered human. A sputter and then a roar. Satisfied the fickle bitch was willing to chauffeur me, I walked towards my apartment to gather the rest of my things and allow the car to warm. She had other plans. Two steps from the door, the engine stopped. Knee deep in snow, staining my pants and freezing my walking twigs, I contemplated remaining still until I was a snowman, eventually trouncing back.

Repeat.

I got on my phone and texted, "Hey A, I'll need a lift today. Can you grab me?"

"*Thumbs up." Her usual early morning response.

We rode in silence; one lane of a five-lane highway etched

clean from other adventurous drivers braving their way to work, slaves to their phone roosters.

The first four hours of my shift, like every first four hours of every 6:00 a.m. shift, went by with me half-asleep. At 10, A, or Arianna to the unlazy texter, and I finished our shift in Terminal 1 and left to go to Terminal 4 to work an 11 to 3.

Terminal 4 is that rival town in high-school. They smell bad. The food selection is worse. They are lazier. Even their water smells like egg-fart. We punched in and reported to the checkpoint supervisor, unhappy to be there.

"You guys are late," she proclaimed. We weren't. She didn't know our names or when our start times were, so she couldn't possibly know. She was just being a bee with chicken-pox.

"Here, put this in the garbage." The ratty-faced Indian, with a methy mouth vault, held out her used Kleenex, prepared to place it in my hand.

"You think I'm going to throw out your used tissue?" I asked, reeling in indignation.

"Yes. I'm in charge of this checkpoint," she proclaimed, acquiring a regal pompousness by the end. She pushed it to-wards me once again. Not that my response would have differed otherwise, but the garbage pail was an equal distance from us. Feigning excitement, I delivered, "In charge of a checkpoint? A real-life checkpoint?"

I casually turned to Arianna and asked, "So, A, what do you think we should eat for lunch?"

The supervisor, Rana, stepped between us. She was steam-ing Willy Beeman. "Don't you turn away when I'm talking to you. Throw this out right now or you're going home."

"Ohhhhhhh nooooo, not homeeeeee," the Grade 6 boy in my head taunted.

Arianna is as anti-authoritarian as they come. Toss in a union and a country with human-rights on her side, and Rana, you've got a problem. Arianna twisted her foot in the way a scolding mother does and delivered equal parts sharp words and harsh barks.

"Don't talk to either of us like that. You're nobody. No one is throwing away your disgusting tissue. Get a life." We began talking again.

"PUNCH OUT!!! PUNCH OUT NOW!!!" she screamed. Screaming, we could handle. I mean inflection of tone? Come on. I've lived through three world wars (Call of Duty world wars): What was some inflection? The problem was not the inflection. It was the grabbing and pulling of Arianna's shoulder. That just wouldn't do.

"Bleeeeeeeeeeeeeeeeeeeeeeeeeeep. Bleeeeeeeeeeeeeeeee-eeeeeeeeeep. Bleeeeeeeeeeeeeeeeeeeeeeeeeeeeeeep, touch me again. Bleeeeeeeeeeeep."

You get the idea. We did punch out. We got paid for it. We were told to do the second half of our shifts in Terminal 1, hence forth.

And ... time to crap where I eat again.

"I'm gonna come in and nap before I go home. I'm too tired to drive," Arianna explained.

"Mmhm," I responded while grinning.

"What?" she said smirking. "I am."

For a couple weeks, leading up to her invitation, we'd started talking about sex more openly. Those conversations led to more personal ones, which led to lingering touches and juvenile flirting.

In my room, she asked, "Do you have any boxers I can wear to sleep?"

It was four in the afternoon. Peter perked up, realizing the score.

"Mmhm."

"Whatttttttttt?"

We crawled into bed. 80's porn composer without his instruments sang, "Bow chica wow wow."

As quickly as it began, it was over.

While at a friend's birthday party, a week later, I received a text from Arianna.

"You probably wonder why I've been ignoring you this week. I thought you had a girlfriend and when I found out you didn't it changed things. It makes me having a boyfriend, so much worse. Sorry. Friends? :)"

I wrote back, "You unscrupulous shrew." I let the text linger for a solid ten minutes, and then I sent another.

"Just joshing. We good!!!! You were a bad lay anyways."

I may as well be a resilient, delinquent jacket, because I was once again off the hook.

# GATWICK, YOU NITWIT

One of, if not the worst, position to do as airport security is randomizer. Not worst as in, difficult, or mentally demanding, or any number of things that a worst job can or should be. It's the worst because it makes me embarrassed to be a human. I recently watched a documentary on apes. Part of the program focused on their abilities to recognize patterns and resolve conflicts on a computer touchscreen, being rewarded for success. So, nothing resembling the ape's accomplishments are happening with humans at the airport.

The randomizer's job is simply to direct passengers to an open door that leads to more important airport security positions. Why can't grown humans figure out which queue has the least amount of people and join it themselves? That's a great question and one I often wonder myself, but they cannot. Not only do we not let them try, but anytime we have, they blow it, royally. Without fail, one line will have thirty people and another will be empty. One or two ambitious people will then tentatively peer over to the open, line-less door and tip-toe over, poking their head in quizzically, as if afraid to catch their mom and dad doing it. A few others will follow their lead, then a few more, and in less than a couple of minutes, the twenty remaining people from the first line will now be in the second. Repeat. At the end of the ape documentary, a human squared off against an ape in competition. Not surprising, the ape won.

The worst aspect of the position is that you're in the line of fire for late or inquiring passengers, and you have nowhere to hide. I hate small talk; small talk with a moron adult wearing a Mickey Mouse sweater is even worse. If I hear, "How has the weather been here?" from someone holding a smartphone with full access and a much more thorough evaluation of how the weather here is, I may ... I don't know. I'm not violent, so probably passive aggressively answer, "Fine."

Because I hate this job, I've found ways to get out of doing it. Much as when I was a kid and I purposely did the dishes wrong every time (yes, I understand there should be no way to mess up wetting and wiping a dish, but I found one), so that my mom wouldn't make me do them anymore, I've found ways to screw the position up.

One day, I strolled to the supervisor podium peppy and with pockets full of treats to munch on while working. The supervisor was new, unaware of my tumultuous randomizing past.

"Please go cover randomizer," he directed.

My pep deflated temporarily, hissing from top cheerleader on the pyramid pep to one of those nondescript girls in the middle; essential load bearing objects. The first few shuffles towards my doom, I dragged ass. Then I realized he'd given me an opportunity. Despite detesting the desolate, mindless position, I'd been given an opportunity to demonstrate my hard-fought reputation as a jackass to him.

Spring forward twenty minutes and he's pulling me inside, asking how I got three passenger complaints in the short time. Mission accomplished.

The feat can be mastered in other ways of course. Not doing anything is one. I say let the heathens organize themselves. That way I'm free to write, or text, or hit on hot female passengers in line. If all goes well, my phone (out of pocket? tsk tsk. Strictly against the rules.) will be heavier, with a new number or two in it before I'm brought in.

One fateful night, I was stuck on randomizer late, nearing the end of my shift. The checkpoint had been dead so only a few processing doors were open and a line grew quickly. Long lines never bode well for the randomizer. I saw an older female passenger, a few lines back, trying to make eye-contact, undoubtedly to lament that she had a flight to catch. Little did she know, I'm a pro at spotting these people in my peripheral, from a distance, and avoiding them at all cost; being as excessive as making small talk with less annoying passengers in order to appear busy. Frazzled, and unfortunately still alive, she shuffled closer. Regrettably, four feet away and close enough to smell the tuna sandwich she'd had for lunch, she was unavoidable no longer.

"Young man," she hissed in my direction, like a snake—a poorly dressed snake. Bad first move. I'm not a young man; I'm an adult. I just act like a young man, and that's only because Lego and GI Joes are really fun to play with.

"Yes," I answered hesitantly. Speaking with her held about the same appeal as eating doody. There are ways I could've escaped the convo. Needing gloves or to speak with someone nearby were classics. But, I saw snake lady as my chance to get inside. Tuna had complainer written all over her round, cobra face and I knew answering the wrong/right way to her dumb questions, would result in her visiting my supervisor for a vent sesh; then I'd get my wish.

My epiphany came mid-way through her shouting, "You guys don't know how to run an airport. You're incompetent morons. Now Gatwick, that country knows how to do it."

I interrupted her, possibly preventing an aneurysm. I slowly articulated, "I'll stop you there ma'am. I think it's best we clarify a few things, before we move this conversation forward. One: I have nothing to do with running the airport. As you can see, my job is to point to a door, indicating people switch from this big line and go stand in one of the smaller lines. At times, this position is even too difficult and mind-boggling for me. I'd have a better chance running a marathon wearing cement boots, than this airport. Second: who are these other guys you are implicating in the running of this airport with me? I'm alone. My colleagues? Do you think we collectively run this airport together?"

She opened her mouth to interrupt. I wasn't done yet, though. I knew I needed a little more gusto for a complaint. "And Gatwick, the country? Do I even bother to explain this to you?"

I liked my rant, thought it was pretty good, in fact, on the spot I began reciting it in my head again, remembering it so I could write it down for my blog. What came next, however, solidified everything. Aghast, and more importantly with hand on hip and right leg pointed out and forward, knee bent like an angry, dapper madam in a 50's sitcom, she said, "Why I never!!" then stormed her way to the longest line.

Ten minutes later, I was relieved from the position because of a complaint. Mission accomplished.

# IUD, IED, SAME DIFFERENCE

I quickly discovered that not everyone I work with speaks the best English. Sorry, bring that back. A lot of the people that I work with don't speak the best English. For passengers already stressed and anxious, reeling on the chaos of a checkpoint, this is probably frustrating. For me, it can lead to some of my favourite work interactions. People insecure about their poor English tend to speak quietly, adding even more confusion. Their speech gives off the audible resolve of a snorkeler with marbles in his mouth trying to speak in Fish. Indians with poor English and bad projection often confuse things more with head bobs and nods. Saying 'no', while making an indifferent head wobble is confusing— even to me—someone who knows the answer to the question. Some of my co-workers refer to people demonstrating these characteristics as ESL (English as a

Second Language). I go a step further and call them NEL (No English Language).

One of the most inarticulate, incomprehensible, lugheads, I've had the misfortune to work with is M. M is from a country. What country, I have no idea. Anytime it seems as if we're making headway on the topic, he gets distracted by obtuse stories about another country. Given his complete inability to pick up on social cues, it's possible his delayed posturing is to avoid admitting he was raised by a wolf, or a fence post.

I was speaking at him, as I did x-ray (I don't mean that guy I used to date called Ray). He stood to my left, pretending to understand me. It could be argued whether he was my bag searcher or lost. A bag appeared, containing a prohibited item. I rested my index finger on the monitor's screen, directly on top of the image of a liquid. I explained, "Everything else is perfectly fine. Just grab that." An obvious, exact specification.

M went above and beyond, pulling open the passenger's large beach bag and rifling through it with vigour. Picture a frantic dog, shaking his head loose from a food sack. The golden retriever's face lit up, he'd found the liquid. Still crouched over the lady's bag, he held the bottle up for me to see. I nodded, said, "Yes, that's it," and gave a dramatic thumbs up. For some reason, his head lowered back inside the bag. A few moments later, he raised a tampon, a universally accepted period plug. The passenger, face beet-red, was standing in front of him, probably to monitor her belongings. Naturally, she attempted to take it from his hand, protecting the two of them from his embarrassing mishap. M didn't see it that way. Years of protecting himself from titty-twisters in school, assisted in his reflective withdrawal. Edging closer to me and creating a wider barrier between the passenger, M asked, in far less comprehensible English than I'm about to write here, "And watzz zizz?"

I knew the tampon was Dracula's teabag, the moment he'd removed it. Furthermore, he was within arms' reach and I could've easily gripped his shirt and yanked him away to explain his idiocy, no problem. But, honestly, why would I? He needed to learn. It was time for M to get the birds and the bees talk. When the lady reached for it again, he protectively shuffled back further, acting like she was trying to get her hands on the detonator to a bomb.

"It's for woman problems," she quietly answered. Her eyes caught mine, pleading for assistance. I wasn't biting. I turned to my screen.

Confused, he asked, "Vat vemen proplems you plan to vake?"

Confused, she replied, "I don't plan on making problems. It's for a woman once a month."

Confused, he demanded, "Vat here. Dont vove."

His giant mitts dangled it delicately, like a scientist would a test tube filled with temperamental fluid, then walked over to me.

"Vat is this?" he asked, shoving it towards my face. I kept up the charade.

Confused, I replied, "No idea, you better ask the supervisor."

Confused, he responded, "Vood idea." Mid-stride, the woman caught his attention and stopped him. She'd removed another tampon from her bag, unwrapped it and was ready for a demonstration.

"Look!!" she urged. With her knees slightly bent, making her undercarriage accessible to her hands, she gestured the insertion of the device. I actually don't know why. If he didn't know what a tampon was, why would he know its second home, or how it was inserted? I doubted that any time in his life, any woman had even let M look at her junk, let alone while she did all that jazz. Perplexity smeared his mug. His expression resembled one you'd expect from a Neanderthal snatched up and thrown in a time machine three million years ago, then plopped into a Comic-Con, present day.

Something clicked with him. Either it was her dramatically cramming a plastic and cloth tube towards her groin in public; the fact that plastic and cloth can't possibly be dangerous; or me laughing hysterically, no longer running the x-ray. The mood changed. He timidly handed it back. Much like moments in any practical joke where someone is a victim at other's expense, I now feared I'd be the next victim, of a much more violent crime. M marched over to me and bent down so his mouth was level with my ear. His deep breathing was unsettling and I instinctively drew from him. He edged closer still, then whispered in my ear, "I vate vu."

# FOUR PENIS WINE

Bouncing through my first year at the airport, I collected some friends. I stayed close with Arianna and Michelle, luckily sans awkward after-humpy. Andy and I remained buddies after training and often maxed out, relaxing all cool, shooting some b-ball outside of the school. I met Big Jazz, an Indian with a propensity for lying and watching full seasons of programs while on "Washroom breaks." There was Ho, the little Asian that could, a down for whatever kinda guy. There was a supporting cast who threw themselves into the mix now and then. Think, Jazzy Jeff on Fresh Prince, or Steve Urkell's cool twin, Stephan, in Family Matters.

Maybe the most monumental addition to my life at the airport was Armando. If monumental isn't the right word, then worst is. Not worst in a bad way. More in the sense that I'm already constantly teetering on the precipice of employment self-destruction through nonsensical mayhem and Armando happens to be that guy, ready with a bulldozer and grenade launcher, to aggressively shove you over.

Armando isn't his real name, and once you read on you'll see why I've changed it. Armando is good-looking, fun, outgoing, and most importantly, not much for working. I'd seen him around, however we didn't actually meet until around my one-year mark.

By way of introduction, he came up to me in a checkpoint and said, "You're white. That makes two of us." I took in my immediate area. He was right. It was my first time being the minority, other than when I went to the Up In Smoke tour in high school and the time my friends stood me up at my small hometown's Chinese restaurant, leaving me alone with a ten-year-old Asian hostess and a cook far too eager to tell me his chicken balls were mouth-watering. I was glad to have Armando as a brother in arms. I figured he could teach me what white privilege got us at the airport. It turns out nothing, but that's okay because Armando wasn't about getting things, he was about taking them.

The first time I noticed his predilection for not working was in an area of the airport, designated for passengers to sleep in when their flights are cancelled or delayed. I guess it wasn't that time, so much as three hours later when he was still there.

"What are you up to?" I asked, more determined to steal his recipe for laziness, than actually knowing what he was doing.

He responded, "I just finished watching the full series of Mad Men."

"Oh, how many episodes did you watch today?"

"All of them."

With that I was smitten; this was to be my work guru.

Somehow, Armando was allowed to be in charge of a checkpoint after 10:00 p.m. That meant for the last two hours of my shift, I got to do nothing. He and I sat inside a private search room and chatted about life outside of the airport, and how we planned on escaping. Sometimes we'd play hacky-sack. Other times we compared drunk stories. Occasionally, we just napped. Before you get any ideas, it was far enough from each other that it wasn't gay; our morning wood barely ever touched.

We'd always sneak out of the airport thirty minutes before the end of our shift, grab our cars then park them out front the building while we ran in to punch out, something we were warned was strictly prohibited. Ya, and so is missing last call for half price wings at Hooters; I've made my decision.

One night, soon after meeting Armando, I pulled a bag from the x-ray machine and dragged it to the end of the line. I identified the owner, a large Jamaican man, and told him to meet me when he'd gathered his belongings. I analyzed the sent x-ray image and identified four large liquids. I pulled them out. The label said Magnum Wine. Underneath the lettering was the silhouette of a man. He had an erection longer than his arm. I asked the passenger, "What exactly is this?" I was curious, not only because I'd never seen the alcohol before, but because I wanted an arms-length erection and the wine seemed to be the ticket.

"It's a drink only sold in Jamaica. It gets you drunk and," he paused to hold up his arm. He flexed it, simulating the phallic outline shown on the bottle. He continued, "Horny!" I was intrigued. The two stated results are favourites of mine.

"How much do you need to drink to get the desired results?" I inquired.

"Not much my brother. Half a bottle and you'll be drunk, led around the bar by your ... " he looked down at my crotch. Feeling awkward, I went into the required speech for oversized liquids.

Dejected, he responded, "Oh, that's too bad man. Like I said, you can't get that stuff here. Enjoy it friend." He slapped me on the back then walked away with a flaccid slunk to his step.

When I dropped the bottles off in the private search room I met Armando, his feet up on a filing cabinet, watching a movie on his phone.

"What you got there slugger?" he asked, peering up from what sounded like a Disney flick.

"Four Penis Wine. Just snagged it off a Jamaican. Says it gives you magical ragers."

He lit up and reached forward; a toddler swiping for teet. "I need me some of that. Throw me one," he urged. I obliged. He cracked the lid, chugged half the bottle then handed me the rest. I followed suit. Ten minutes later I was tipsy but unfortunately with no discernible boner. We crushed another a few minutes later. The checkpoint was due to close and we assumed we were done work for the night —erections and drunk couldn't get us in trouble.

We were wrong. Armando got a call on his phone from a supervisor saying the Colorado Avalanche had a late charter flight and we were needed to reopen the checkpoint and push them through, alone.

Armando sat down on x-ray and I went to the front to scan boarding passes. I was tipsy. I looked at Armando, he looked trashed. Some of the Avs I recognized at a glance, others looked like high school students on a snowboard trip. Patrick Roy approached me, his face identifiable as one slightly hidden behind a goalie mask on a poster hanging on my bedroom wall for over two years when I was in my early teens.

Beaming, I asked the legend, "Mr. Roy, how you doing?"

He smiled and handed me his boarding pass.

"Buddy, look! Hey look!" Armando peskily whispered from his seat. I stared sharp darts at him and asked, "What? Can't you see I'm having an in-depth conversation with NHL legend and Stanley Cup champion Patrick Roy?"

"Yesssss … ..But look." He jabbed at a bulge in his pants. "I've got a boner." He burst out laughing. I looked at Patrick who was looking at Armando pointing at his bone job. He walked away. I glared down at Armando then pointed at my own wonderful stiffy. "Me too!! I don't know if it's from the Four Penis Wine or from seeing Patrick Roy!"

A few years later, half-cut, I stumbled into a grocery store on Pedro Island in Belize. I entered the store with the intention of grabbing some Red Bull; a little pick-me-upper after an exhausting eight hours of day-drinking. I was unwilling to shut it down at seven in the evening. After chatting up two sexy girls from Tennessee on the inappropriately named, secret, Secret Beach, who made my friends and I promise we'd come out later in the evening; I had motivation to last.

"They don't have Red Bull on the island," my friend, Mark, announced from behind me. Mark's generally intelligent and competent, the exception being when he's drunk. That happened to be the state he'd been in since we left home three days prior. I ignored him and perused a large refrigerator. Noticing this, he continued.

"I told you, they don't have it on the island."

Mark is Irish. Locals speak English but with a slow, Patois-like slang. To them, I'm guessing drunk Mark sounded like a vacuum cleaner with a marble stuck in it. Something caught my eye. The logo rang a bell. I inched closer. Could it be? The seal breaking of the fridge-door sent a nearly blinding fog fleetingly floating towards shelves and momentarily disrupted my view of my potential treasure. The mist may have been the veil being lifted by a fridge magician ending an illusion meant to deceive me. But, no, no, the familiar bottle remained cradled on the shelf. Reminiscent of Gollum, I ecstatically extended my hand towards my precious. I examined the bottle, ascertaining whether it was the treasure I sought. The colouring matched my memory. The illustrations slightly different but full of eroticism and implied erections. I'd found it, my illusive Four Penis Wine.

Careful to shelter the bottle from a grabby Mark, I presented the intriguing label.

"You see this nob gobbler? This is the elixir of the Gods. Four Penis Wine. The hundred-year-old bottle of Moet of the malt wine industry. Stick with me and I'll take you to the promise land."

"Huh?"

"Imbecile. It's boner drink. Viagra in a bottle. The perfect combination of erection fuel and energy drank."

"Huh?"

"Where am I losing you Mark? Drink this and you get boners and have the endurance to keep going alllll night. We confiscated it from a Jamaican man at the airport once and my friend and I drank it. Ten minutes later we were drunk and rocking throbbers. It's miraculous liquid."

Belize's Four Penis Wine was to be no exception.

# BRITTLE LITTLE
# BIRD BRAIN

Inside an airport security-screening checkpoint, it's well-understood by employees that passengers will have inquiries. We get it, you have questions. You're a little baby bird poking your beak through the eggshell, spilling forth into the world for the first time. Unlike the stingy Spiderman and his, 'Everyone gets one', policy, we'll even allow multiple questions. Heck, go ahead and verbally hiccup poorly structured, naive questions. As I said, we get it. Our default setting is an assumption that passengers lack flying experience. Questions about something you've just been told seconds before though, does warrant a little less patience and often a sigh.

Questions such as, "Does a pen count as liquid?" often elicits a day-dreamed kick to the nuts and power-bomb (I can say bomb, but you better bite your tongue if you wanna get on this plane). Some questions are obviously more deserving of voodoo dolls, made to guarantee the passenger receives the pain and suffering they bestowed on the screener, than others.

Lucky for those readers hoping to read about idiots, but completely detrimental to my ever-receding free-flowing ventricles, patience and hairline, I receive a fair share of these questions. Movies such as 'It' and 'Paranormal Activity' don't scare me (who am I kidding, they do). What I might do to the next person who asks, "Me too?" after I've just announced, "EVERYBODY!! take off their shoes," does.

To this day, the dumbest question I've heard from a passenger was in response to, "Do you have anything sharp or breakable in your bag?" The stout, ogre-looking man raised his eyebrows in thought. His keg-shaped head swivelled around the checkpoint as if searching for someone with more than the dime-sized brain he had rattling around his cranium, to help him answer. His mouth flopped open then formed an 'O', mimicking the breathing reflexes of a guppy. He closed it, thought again. Finally, he spat out, "Do my bones count as breakable?" Initially, I didn't process the question. I've grown accustomed to dumb questions at work and have defensively acquired a method of glazed-over listening and response.

I began to say, "You," but got caught on the U for about five seconds. I came out of my trance and continued, "You are kidding ... right?" I laughed, kinda along with him, although he wasn't laughing, just standing there like a dink. I thought he'd take the cue and join in; allowing us both to pretend the question was a joke. I'd deemed him the goofy kid on the playground, so frail everyone awarded him a free pass from atomic wedgies.

His surprise expression surprised me.

"No," he answered.

I asked, "Your bones are in your body, not in your bag. Correct?" I really hoped he didn't have bones removed from his body in his bag. Although, if he was some kinda killer, contemplating murdering me for insinuating he was an idiot, through condescension, his missing supportive bones may help in my defence.

He squinted, indicating a mental scan through his bag. Finally, he responded, "All my bones are in my body, yes."

To make sure, I asked, "There are no breakable bones in your bag?"

With a satisfied grin, he answered, "No, they are in my body."

"Your breakable bones are in your body?" I continued, determined to make sure, and also to take the piss out of him.

"Yes."

"Okay. Great. Moving on. Is there anything sharp or breakable in your bag?"

He answered, "No," then caught himself, demonstrating he'd almost made a dire mistake. "Maybe."

Friggin maybe? Maybe? Ahhhhhhh.

"Good enough. Have a nice day."

Exasperated, I urged him from my sight with a wrist flick. Inside, I obviously thought, "If your bones are as breakable as you imply, and you're as much of a Neanderthal as you seem, I wouldn't be surprised if you regularly break femurs and phalanges forgetting how to walk."

Of course, I didn't say any of this—I'm a consummate professional (notttttt). I waited until he was out of earshot, then I mumbled it under my breath, then I told my fellow workers, then I wrote about it here in a soon to be acclaimed book.

# I'D LIKE TO BUY A QUESTION MARK, PAT

Sometimes, the dumb questions I'm asked by passengers aren't even technically dumb questions. They are words, delivered flat, short of their intended goal, and obviously influenced by the New England Patriot's; Deflate Gate.

In my opinion, inflection of tone is very important. Something that drives me bonkers— absolutely up-the-wall-insane—is when a passenger says one word, no inflection, and really to no one in particular. "Shoe," is a prime example. "E7," another. "Watch," gets thrown around a lot. The intention is obviously there. The person wants to know something about that item, but why be lazy? If you can't make the effort to turn your word into a question, I'm not going to formulate an answer.

That's exactly what I do when I'm in a good mood. I look at the person like they're a dumb-dumb, just saying random words out loud, and shrug, as if to say, "Congratulations you have shoes," or, "Well done, you said necklace without any hiccups," much the way you do to little children when they brag of an accomplishment you can achieve drunk and with your eyes closed. When I'm in a bad mood, or feeling coocoo bananas, things change. Here's where I like to employ sarcasm.

A passenger approaches the divest station. I'm either helping someone else or not paying attention; the not paying attention one is most likely. A swashbuckling business man delivers, "Shoes," with Tourette-like sporadicity; speaking over an elderly lady laboriously urging what little wind she has remaining in her sagging lungs towards her toothless gum-box to ask where she needs to place her jar of mints. Sure, I know what he means. He wants to know if he needs to remove his shoes. But, writing, he needs to remove his shoes, was easy, and arguably typing is more difficult than speaking (or in Stephen Hawkins' case, equally as difficult). So, why can't he speak those words; and why can't he get my attention with a polite, "Sir" Or a, "Beautiful squire, may you address the conundrum bestowed upon me in part due to multiple rule changes, my ignorance, and my infrequency of travelling, please?" I'm a real softy for medieval jargon.

How do I respond to shoe guy? Usually, I don't. Sometimes I look away. Other times I give him a dirty look. When I do respond, I may lecture. It's not uncommon to hear me scold like, "Sir, it's impolite to interrupt others." Or, "Sir, please formulate a question if you have a question." Or, "Sir, see this knife? One more outburst from you and you won't be able to see it because it'll be in your back." The passenger usually squints their eyes, confused and offended. My stoic face, reminiscent of a veteran military sergeant, deters any combative retaliation. In some cases, they right their wrong. Most other times, they just repeat 'shoes' again, a sad reiteration which takes seconds off my life. Shoes isn't the only single syllable utterance void of inflection required to complete a meaning spat at me. I get: watch; belt;

phone; and pockets, constantly.

One method I use to tease lazy passengers, is to engage them in a rousing game of word association. Here's an example:

"Phone."

"AT&T, Telus, Rogers, Broken, E.T. blank, home, word in a Beyoncé and Gaga song."

They say, "International."

I respond, "Roaming, travel, conflicts."

"Watch."

"A dog. A show. Out here I come, you spin me right round baby right round, like a record baby right round right round."

I also like to pretend what they said is not what they said.

"Shoes."

"Ma'am, I'd love to look after your kids this weekend, but I have a lot on my plate; maybe some other time. Thanks for considering me though."

"Change."

"You're absolutely right, best outfielder in the league; can't get enough of the guy."

The moral of the rant is ... hmmm I'll find it ... oh yeah, there it is. If you can't be bothered to ask a proper question, I'm not going to give you a proper answer.

# BACKSTREET BRAWLING BABY

There are a number of people that I work with, who I can't stand. I've got a top three, a top five, and even a top ten. I haven't bothered making a top twenty, but it wouldn't be a problem. Number one by a long way is Craig. This is not his real name of course, I don't need that lunatic knowing I've written about him; he's relentless. He's liable to hunt down Trump, plead his case, and with his annoying persistence, have me Guantanamo-Bayed. I thought about using it, just to screw with the prick.

There are so many stories I could tell about the guy—so I will. He's the only constant annoyance and stress I have at work. If he's in the lunchroom, I leave. Washroom, the same. If it didn't cost me a pay cheque, I wouldn't be found in the same building as the guy.

Here's a description of Craig to help visualize the stories:

He walks like an erect penis, given an undeserved position of power. His face also resembles a dick. In fact, it resembles what I assume the dick of Burt, from Sesame Street's Burt and Ernie, looks like. He swears … well like a sailor. It's obvious that using cuss words is a defence mechanism for having the vocabulary of a toddler. He once pushed an emergency alarm on himself.

He tells people he's had nightmares about missing things on the line and woken up with such a bad conscience that he's considered telling management, instigating a review of surveillance footage to determine if his dream was actually a premonition. I assure you, his only resemblance to Joseph, the fancy, multiple-vibrant-coloured coat wearer, is his brother's hatred for him. No doubt his receding hairline is the result of the continuous stress he feels over every little thing that happens, pertaining to airport security, including but not limited to EVERY LITTLE THING!! Either that or his hair is just trying to get away from his annoying mouth and stupid penis face.

Also—most telling of his personality—he's one of those guys who wears a watch with a Velcro wrist band and is constantly tightening it, as if somehow his wrist grows smaller and larger as the day goes on. To make matters worse, the watch is definitely for kids. He wears glasses, maybe not even out of necessity; but, at least, partially to diminish the fact that he's a complete moron. He's got that shoulder and head pushed back so you force a double chin and authoritative voice-thing going on. He projects everything he says as if it's commonly accepted fact, but as he's saying it to someone who doesn't believe him; a condescending pompousness. Ummm, I guess that's about it. Oh, he's married to a FOB Asian I'm guessing was mail-ordered.

### Story 1. October 15th, 2018.

Setting: A tranquil, harmonic lunchroom.

Scene: Eight people enjoying chilled conversation and their lunches. In walks Craig.

Outside voice, nine out of ten loud, in a small, quiet room: "You know why everyone hates customs?"

Side note: They don't. I don't think I've ever heard anyone say they hate customs. Custom's officers are some of the most indifferent people I've met. Plus; their job is to stop drugs and bad things coming into their country. Even if they were dicks, who could blame them?

Before anyone can comment, (No one was going to anyways. When he speaks people automatically avoid eye contact and pretend to be occupied) he continues. "Because they shove their hands up everyone's asses all the time."

Side note 2: Not true. They never do. The procedure, if they suspect someone of having something in their bum, is to feed them laxatives and have them sit on a toilet with a strainer at the bottom. I don't know one person who's ever said customs put their hand in their bum. Maybe he mistook them for puppeteers. No one in the lunchroom says a word. I left, muttering about what a jackass he is as I walked by him.

**Story 2. Some other time.**

Here's the Grand Poobah of Craig's mishaps. He was working bag search. The other bag searcher was sent a key-chain with a mini set of brass knuckles on it: a novelty gift store item. I'll reiterate here, IT WASN'T A BAG SENT FOR SEARCH TO THE DICK OF BURT. Unless asked for advice, there's no reason to interfere with someone else search. I bet you can guess what happened next. That's right, the semen involved himself.

"What have we got here?" he stated, chin tucked into a pushed forward chest, arms erect like his dick over evaporated water (this is a joke illustrating the fact that Craig is so enthusiastic about airport security that he'd get turned on by water – airport security's arch nemesis – evaporating). The other bag searcher, Tom, shook his head, surrendering on the spot to

Craig's involvement. Tom left the area, privy to all that's Craig. He stood next to me in the area where Craig should have been, but wasn't, because he's dumb. Tom, privy to Craig's nonsense, announced in my ear, "Craig's about to do something dumb. Watch."

We did. He did.

Craig began, "Sir, what have you got planned for this weapon here?" He shook the tiny key chain, bobbing his head in disbelief in succession with its metallic rattle.

Indifferently, the passenger responded, "Decoration." Craig's rebuttal came quickly, harsh and suggestive. "You think something that can hurt someone is decoration?"

Now, I don't know if you've ever watched Law and Order-Special Victims Unit, but the man answered the way Ice-T's character does when presented with something confusing: squinting, staring off into the distance, and something like, "You mean like a painting? Or a side table? Or an antique sword?" The answers seemed abstract, but dammit, the guy was right. What can't be used to hurt people? My first love hurt me by offering an alternative relationship where she jagged off other dudes and I wept like a puss-filled wound in my parent's basement. That's neither here nor there really, but man that crap hurt.

Craig's face went the colour he'd use for the majority of his drawings of decapitated bunnies.

"No, not like an antique sword," he lashed out. "I mean yes, like one." For some reason, Craig then looked at Tom and I, as if we were somehow going to offer him up a lifeline. Confused dog, keep your head down, get out your compass, and follow Google Maps; you'll find it.

The passenger, who looked perplexed, bored, and sexy in a three-piece suit that Harvey from Suits couldn't look better in, asked, "Are we done here?" With his mouth open and head still gazing foliage bound, Craig answered, "No," then went about formulating those never elusive irrational thoughts of his into a more-or-less incoherent sentence, "Do you have a baby with you?"

You betcha, Tom and I laughed, although we listened with renewed interest, in suspense about what in high heavens a baby had to do with anything. You're about to get some insight into the mind of a madman; brace yoself foo.

"No," the passenger answered. Bring out the generator or large-lunged uncle—Craig's deflated. Not deflated enough to miss enlightening us all with the reason for his seemingly brash question though.

"Well if you did, I'd have pressed the alarm because the baby could wear those and punch people."

Aghast. A-Friggin-Ghast, I snorted. What else can you do when some absolute maniac suggests that a tit-feeding infant might strap on some brass knuckles, attached to a key chain, and go Chuck Norris on a flight of unsuspecting passengers and flight attendants? As if a baby, so violence-craved that he requires his weapon of choice to be sheathed by his father, and kept out of his reach in a cottony pocket of sleek slacks, wouldn't have unleashed his hellish fury recently enough that the remnants of blood and flesh left from victims would have been dripping from them like a morbid winter nativity scene.

Finally, I involved myself in the procession.

"Sir, you're free to go. Continue to keep that barroom-brawling baby of yours at home; we don't need any trouble round des parts. Much obliged."

He laughed and left. Craig ... Craig said some crap, but I absolutely did not listen. I turned to Tom and said, "Now you know why his mother and I tried to abort him."

Tom inquired, "You're his father?"

I responded, "Nope."

# BACKSTREET BRAWLING PORN STARS

It's late. A female passenger in leggings and a tight top approaches. She walks through the metal detector machine and alarms. I send her back. She tries again, once more alarming. I take her to the private search room and run the scanning wand down her body, hoping to find where the non-discreet, metal object is hidden. Mid-bum, I get my answer.

"Ma'am," I begin. "Have you hidden something in your pants?"

She responds, "I'm not sure what you are talking about, officer. Perhaps you should check."

I rip a hole in the middle of her leggings, pull down her underwear and find a metal butt plug. Yes, this is standard, late-night protocol. Next, you guessed it; we have aggressive sex on every inch of a metallic search table.

Was that reality? No. Believe it or not. It was in a porno I saw. So, I guess it was kinda reality, but a reality where I'm lying in my bed, nearly-naked, with a tablet set up next to me on one side, a box of Kleenex on the other, and an air of erotic self-discovery about to condensate above. TMI?

Sex tapes. Got your attention, don't I. Well I should. Tape used for sex is the best; with enough of it, you can keep anyone quiet – cue creepy, exaggerated laugh. My airport employs roughly two-thousand screening officers, varying in age from eighteen to one guy who I'm pretty sure is dead and his corpse reflectively zombies itself to work each day. Through Whats-App and Facebook, groups of employees can exchange shifts and/or work-related information. WhatsApp, as you may know, is also a place where friends make groups in which they exchange more personal messages. You're probably thinking right now, that I'm going to write how I've inserted inappropriate messages or videos into the group. You'd be wrong, but I like the idea. I'll probably do it later tonight.

No, I wanted to discuss how an older, black man whom everyone assumes is homosexual, once "accidentally" put some BBW porn into the group—and how, soon after, a BBW I work with accidentally posted a video of her mixing the ol' down-under DJ equipment. Now, five years into my employment, a young, attractive female, sent the Mona Lisa of accidental group chat sex messages: a solo video highlighted by an inner-thigh rendition of Niagara Falls.

Although lovely distractions from the monotonous, "Urgently giving away 1400 to 2200," the WhatsApp mishaps aren't what I'm hoping for when I type: Airport Security, into my porn search bar. For those curious, my expectations for the search end with a video, featuring a sexy and barely clothed female approaching someone else clothed and a male. A very brief exchange of words takes place before the female is stripped and sex with a minimal amount of blow-jobbing takes place. I'm not picky though. If it's a female security officer and a male passenger, I'll live.

Working x-ray in the international checkpoint, my work life and my porn watching life came together. For once, not in the handicapped bathroom. Came together, get it? Har Har.

X-ray is an important position on the screening line, mostly because it's the only one where you sit. Secondly, you get to tell someone else what to do pertaining to searching bags ... and they have to do it, no matter how ridiculous. This is obviously annoying if you're in fact not the operator, but the person having to search the stupid bags. Don't worry though, there will always be time to get even with these people. Oh, and the x-ray position is technically where you'd catch any weapons someone's attempting to infiltrate, and I guess that's kinda important to some.

When viewing the x-ray images, you're given a window into peoples' lives. I can easily tell someone's a hooker by the five pairs of heels, ten bras, zillion panties, and enough baby wipes to overflow a commercial toilet, in her carry-on, for a weekend flight to Las Vegas. Likewise, you can tell which businessmen are cheating when you see their wedding ring and picture of their kids sitting next to a jumbo-sized box of condoms and a lipstick-stained dress shirt. Personally, I like to make up a life for the people after seeing what's in their carry-on. Most are boring, or the items are indistinguishable, but you do get the odd few that blow your mind.

"An adult with giant crayons in his bag ... hmm," I pondered out loud. "You thinking he's got kids or that he's one of those strange addiction guys who puts colouring tools in his anus then walks around with a piece of them shoved hidden in his nose all day?" I asked Jim, my bag searcher one day. He peered at the man, then the x-ray image, then me.

Finally, he responded, "This is what you called me over for? I thought you had a bag for me to search?" So, it was settled, he was definitely the former.

One night, I was sitting on x-ray, minding my own business. I had company-known tattle-tale— and my worst enemy— Craig, as my bag searcher and decided to make him work. I sent business cards to check while saying to him, "Those are business cards. Make sure they're business cards."

"What else could they be?" he asked, surprised by my request.

"Oh, they can only be business cards," I replied. "But go check them anyways."

The goody-goody is known for watching people over their shoulders while they x-ray, then tattling when they do something wrong. Needless to say, I wanted him as far away from me as possible at all times. Within thirty minutes, I had sent him to check a mug I guaranteed was a mug, a watch I told him I'd be willing to bet a million dollars was a watch and a bag with only clothes because, as I said, "You never know; but I do know. There are only clothes in there. Go check anyways though."

From my seat, I saw the passengers as they approached. Two petite, sexy blondes walked up. They had too much makeup, bleach, and clothes (too many for me because they were smokinnnnn hot. They were both wearing short shorts and belly tops). The equipment in front of me became relevant only to shield my boner. Craig came over and asked if the cellphone he was holding was, in fact, the cellphone I'd sent him to search minutes before.

I didn't look at him or the item while replying, "Yeah, yeah, that's it. Go away." I didn't need him killing my mood, or boner or being in proximity to either. As the girls walked through, I lost sight of them because the x-ray machine was blocking my view. I thought, 'first you give me cancer and now this, you damn x-ray machine'. I hadn't looked at my monitor for a good few minutes, so had a glance to make sure everything was alright. It was not. Rolling across my screen was a plethora of prohibited items. I saw handcuffs, brass knuckles, brass knuckles with a blade, whips, and a few knives. Surrounding the deadly weapons were dildos, almost as if placed there to soften the image. I peered over my screen at the girls and they were smiling, because why wouldn't you smile when you are that gorgeous?

The routine for an emergency is to call over your EDT and supervisor as a second and third opinion in confirming the threat and then to press an alarm. Brass knuckles with knives are pretty discernible from the usual pens and a book. There was absolutely no need for another opinion. Not to mention, I hated my EDT and wanted him far away. As for my supervisor, earlier in my shift he'd told me he was at a bachelor party all weekend. Still buzzing off tequila shots, I didn't need him freaking out when he saw triples of all the prohibited items. I pressed the alarm and followed emergency procedures. I stood up to talk to the girls, taking the time to look behind them and see who the freak psychopath carrying the bag of no-no items was. The only people left in line were old, frail and shaky. They weren't in any position to be holding razor-sharp blades to each other's necks during a home invasion role-playing game. They barely looked as if they should be out of the old-age home, alone. I looked back at the two cute blondes. Surely they couldn't be the owners of the bag of horrors?

The police arrived a few minutes later and confirmed the bag was, in fact, the girls'. The two giggled and continued smiling, recounting the fake snuff porn scene they'd filmed earlier that day. I inched closer, subtly inserting myself into the conversation. My co-worker, William, had a different plan. Six-foot-five, tall, black, muscular and beautiful, William is the man at work women swoon over. If they don't, he just picks them up, carries them home, and does push-ups topless in front of them until they do. He jovially galloped over, literally sliding into the conversation.

"Ladies, how's it going?"

William hadn't seen the image so didn't know the girls were psycho murderers.

"These boys bothering you?" he asked, using a casual over-the-shoulder thumb point to identify the cops. The blondes giggled. I listened for "Bow chica wow wow." Not willing to relinquish his position as host of the arrest, William continued. "These gentlemen arresting you two for being too sexy?" Man the guy's good. I should be writing this down. They giggled again. It was my chance to spring into action. I wanted me a piece of that pussy pie. Ewwww. As debonair as I could muster, I added, "They have illegal weapons. They're bad women," in the way an old gay-guy Queen living in Brooklyn would.

My internal 'cool' register, screamed, *WHAT THE COCK-MUNCH WAS THAT YOU IMBECILE!!?*

The first sentence was muted by their conversation and by the bad women part; my voice had dropped seventy-three octaves and came out like the pedophile from Family Guy. The group of five collectively gave me a disgusted, nice-try buddy, look and continued speaking among themselves. Ashamed, I returned to my seat at x-ray. I saw Craig posturing a few feet from the action, physicking himself up to join the conversation. He was my hope. I'd be whacking off to the porn stars later and didn't need my memory psychologically shaming me to limp. If Craig just acted himself I'd be off the hook. The stupidity he spat generally superseded my own.

The group was in comfortable banter, looking like old friends. Craig lingered around the edge of their circle, hands on hip, head chicken bobbing. He pushed forward and said something I couldn't hear. The body language told me I'd gotten my wish. Craig slunk away, hands in pocket, shaking his head. Walking towards me, I came to the sad realization that if he joined me I had no choice but to willingly accept him for once; we were temporarily connected by rejection.

As we watched, shrouded in shame, the cops let the females off with a slap on the wrist (I'm sure the two didn't mind, already numbed from whips and knives). The bad items were confiscated and I fired back up the x-ray, forced to finish my shift before I saw the two again, on my home computer screen.

# ABOUT TIME

W hen I tell people I work airport security, second only to the question, 'what's the weirdest thing you've seen in the x-ray machine,' is, 'do you see a lot of celebrities'? The answer is yes. Nearly every day. Between celebs and athletes, I pretty much work at the Betty Ford clinic. However, it's not as glamorous as all that. Usually I see them from a distance, or because a co-workers just said, "Did you see P. Diddy? He just came through," and I catch the back of his Himalayan, child-skin jacket and entourage of guys who, if instead of slacking in school and ending up as human shields, receiving sloppy seconds as tips, practised dunking a ball, would be making millions working one-hundred minute weeks.

I get asked, "Have you met George Clooney?" Often. I have ... kinda, sorta. His magnificent aura did once project in my direction, urging my eyes towards his radiating glow, nudging a man-lust never before stirred. The hunk kept a smile his whole entire time in the checkpoint. Like twenty-minutes of smiling and comfortingly gripping people in a cross between how your mother held you as a baby and the way a Baileys and coffee on a cold winter morning in front of the fireplace at the cottage feels.

Sports teams come through a lot, returning from games or heading on the road. They're nearly always nice. Possibly because a lot of them know that if not for running faster than a Porsche, they'd be standing in our shoes. Celebrities are fifty/fifty. John C Reilly: Champ. Dude dresses like an 1800s plantation owner and chats to you like a bestie. Lesser known brother of a reality TV famous family of imbeciles: Don't tell anyone, but he was on drugs when I met him; and a dick, and his breath smelled, and I hate him. Margot Robbie: Is there a way to write that emoji with eyes shooting hearts out of them? In the words of Wayne, from Wayne's World, "Shawingggggg." Britney Spears: It's Britney bitch!! Channing Tatum and his Wife: Short and sweet.

There are two celebrities I've had interactions with more than any other. Bill Chill (not his real name) is the first. I'm rather torn on the guy. On one hand, I like his one-man 'Tuesday Morning Podcast' podcast, a lot of his stand-up, and interviews. On the other, I hate everything he's ever done the couple times I've experienced him coming through airport security. My one hand wants to shake his hand and the other wants to smack those ginger pubes he calls a beard off of his face.

I'm generally not starstruck. The only real hiccups I've had while talking to celebs or sports stars usually gravitates around them being so hot that I jizz in my pants and stand silent because I'm worrying whether my red face and quivering gives me away. Reciting lines, being good-looking but short, and being rich for doing so, doesn't overly impress me.

My first interaction with the aptly last-named Chill should have been prototypical. Most of our officers are pretty chill themselves when it comes to celeb interactions. With a demographic Kim K's body explains perfectly, our older and younger brown employees make up her tits and ass and everyone else her stomach area. We are top and bottom heavy. A clever metaphor? Or a way for me to justify picturing Kim's body? We all know the answer to that one. Basically, with a division in age and race far outside of Bill's standard demographic, he walked through uninterrupted; translucent both in skin tone and fame. Yet when he arrived to me, on bag search, he was perturbed, agitated.

"Hello sir," I began. "I just have to have a look in your bag." Despite his wearing a paperboy hat, I recognized Mr. Chill right away, his clever disguise foiled. I also noticed that he seemed angry. I also know Irish people can get moody without drink. Since airport security creates, at least, a pause in being on the drink, he might have been in a drinkless sad/upset world; I empathized. Here's a little aside. Did you know that the difference between empathy and sympathy is proximity? Well it is. You need to be in the person's presence to be empathetic. Huh, there ya go.

So ol' Bill approached. I said my spiel and began to search. This is where Bill chose not only to look like a dick, but act like one.

"Is this really necessary?" he brusquely asked while peering intently at nothing on the ground to his right, a gesture made by socially disrespectful people with no patience.

I asked in turn, "Airport security? Checking of bags, or yours in particular?"

His head sharply swivelled. He stared at me through the top of his eyes. In the fashion of a tough-guy hero in an edgy saves the day film, Bill responded, "Me."

"You part of the category everyone?" I asked.

"I ... "

I cut him off with, "Yes. Yes you are."

"I'll be over here then," he stated while walking towards a wall, about ten feet away. Alright, first, there's no seats by the wall, so what kinda autistic comforting bullcrap are those shenanigans? Second, no you're not. I said it; and I'll say it again. I hope I don't have to because I don't like repeating myself, but I will ... oh I will (sorry, had to).

Now at level eight angry, he slunk back to me.

"Go," he instructed.

We know my opinion on random words void of inflection needed to ascertain the words purpose.

"Where?" I asked.

Perplexed, he asked, "What?"

I'd heard the routine before.

"Who."

Bill squinted and asked, "What?" again.

"It's *when* Bill," I offered.

Bill got it, and played along ... maybe. "When are you going to check my bag?"

Not what I had in mind, but sure.

"Now. Now works for me. Anything sharp or breakable in your bag, Bill?"

Yes, yes I did finish the question condescendingly with Bill. Sue me. Bill me.

"Why the hell would I have anything sharp or breakable in my carry-on bag?" he spat.

Feigning deep thought, I replied, "Good question."

He looked at me like, now we're getting somewhere. We were, but nowhere he wanted to go. Time to answer dumb rhetorical questions.

"I'll start with sharp. I think we can all agree that the tip of pens are sharp." I paused to scan an audience that didn't exist. "Exactly. So, why would you have a pen in your bag?" I knew the answers. I'm not bragging or anything, but I mean there really are limited things a normal person can use a pen for. Still, I'm polite and like to incorporate the audience so they feel like participants, not students. I waited for Bill. If I was a dart board, I'd have been impressed.

"Awkwardddd," I mumbled under my breath. From Bill's side of the search table came more sighs than a Raphael convention.

Making things uncomfortable for jerk head passengers is fun for and a hobby of mine. That being said, I am susceptible to the occasional flushing of embarrassment, red face, and shortness of breath spells that come with it. Whenever this happens, I usually spit out something quick and move away from the situation. Aggressive stares or large audiences are usually the catalyst.

I felt the red ascending from my chest, my little heart pumping it past my 'meh' sculpted chest, engulfing a neck insistent on bunching under my chin, and finally to cheeks working overtime to stay cute and youthful forever. I wouldn't hack it as one of Ashton's less famous lackeys on 'Punked', I'd crack mid-prank and ruin it all, similar to what Ashton's done with his career choices.

My charade was up. I sifted through Bill's bag bashfully, zipped it, mumbled something about pens and turned my back to the whole situation. Bill, perplexed, and still a stiff dick, rearing to spit, venomously asked, "Are you done?"

Articulately, and a tad selfish to whomever may want to use positive acknowledgement in the future, only to find out I'd taken them all from the storage closet, I answered, "Yep, yeah, mmhmm, yes," then walked away. There was a garbage bin I needed to pretend to scrutinize in awkward distraction.

The other celebrity I've had quite a few interactions with is the love of my life. My crush on her probably started around Regina George O'clock. I love Rachel McAdams!!! She's wonderful!!! And, adding to her allure, she has a knack for finding and wooing time travellers.

The first time I met her was while doing randomizer,

ambitiously directing people to short lines. Angelically, she approached. She's radiant. Petite, and the cutest little thing I'd ever done seen. My face went red. I stuttered, Hi," about thirty times. I think I blacked out. Next thing I knew, I was spitting out this nonsense: "Do you like Disney movies?"

What in tarnation was I thinking? Did I imagine we'd bond over tales of mermaids and dogs eating spaghetti? Maybe if it went well enough, I'd suggest the two of us re-enact the scene in the cafeteria? I don't even know that much about Disney movies, the above is almost my extent. That and the one about the gypsy thief who talks to birds.

Luckily, instead of puking on my face in disgust, she giggled. A real life giggle!! A glorious jiggling of the funny bone!! My confidence went from negative 700 (basically me feeling like a leper *sans* nearly every body part but one eye and a tooth who'd just crapped his tattered pants) to a 7 billion (You don't need a plane to take you back to Hollywood, anymore Rachel, I'm so high with joy you can hop on my back and I'll fly you).

A few seconds later, the perfect angel slowly walked away. Most likely to escape the awkwardness of me standing there grinning at her, nearly drooling and dopey-eyed. The next passenger walked up and asked, "What line should I join?" knocking me out of my psychotic – watch-Rachel-walk-away-stare.

"I don't care, sir!" I responded. "They're all the same. Now move along."

What kind of man interferes with another man awkwardly watching the woman of his dreams leave?

Rachel story #2 coming soon!!

# EIO

"I'm moving in a week. Gary has already moved out so he can avoid paying the landlord last month's rent and for all the crap he's broken. You guys think I should throw a banger?"

The lethargic crew perked up, motivated more by a reason for drinking their faces off than identifying prohibited items.

"Hellssss yes," Jazz responded.

Armando sprang from his slunk position and chimed in with, "Do you have a security deposit?"

If you'd told me that I was going to mention having a huge, moving out party to Armando, then asked what I thought his response would be, it was that.

"I do Armando. Leave your chainsaw at home."

Disappointment crossed his face and he slid back down the blue lounge chair.

Maria contributed, "I can bring a goat."

"Why, can you bring a goat? How can you bring a goat? What goat?" I asked, unbahhhhhlieving.

Straight-face and stoic, she answered, "I'm Muslim."

We all shrugged.

Jazz announced, "Buddy, I've got an idea. Since you're from the country, and Maria is bringing a goat." I interrupted to say, "It hasn't been decided if the goat is coming." Maria shook her head and said, "Oh the goat is coming." Jazz went on. "Since you're from the country, and since Maria is bringing a goat, why don't we bring more animals and call it EIO fest?"

With peaked interest, I asked, "EIO fest?"

"Yeah, like Ol' McDonald had a farm, EI, EI, O."

Collectively, the four of us shook our heads in approval. EIO fest was born.

"You should have let me bring a chainsaw," Armando said through sad head-shakes as he and I lifted a couch and carried it outside. We dropped it on the edge of my driveway, next to the majority of my apartment's furniture. "I don't trust you with a butter knife when you're drunk. There's no way I'd let you bring a gas-powered saw into my house when you are." He looked at me with fury.

Guest started arriving around seven and by ten the small, basement apartment was packed. In Gary's room we'd set up tables for beer pong and flip-cup and in the living room, DJ equipment and coolers full of booze. Everywhere was designated the weed-smoking zone and the corner closest to the speakers the "girl dancing with herself because she's really high on molly and no one wants to dance with her because she's the only one on it," corner.

The cops broke the party up sometime after midnight, siting drunken street Frisbee, couch smashing (by, you guessed it, Armando) and noise. The party was again broken up by cops at around two, this time with pre-written tickets shown to demonstrate the urgency of the threat.

I woke up to an apartment sticky with spilled booze, seven passed out co-workers, one guy I didn't know, and two hours until my work shift. I clumsily and slowly put on my uniform, drank water from the tap, and shuffled out my door. I stepped over my friend Kim Jung, sprawled out like the chalk outline of a murder victim, dense, yellow puke forming the appearance of a cartoon voice bubble next to his mouth, and made my way to my car.

Knowing Armando was supposed to be working, I messaged him, "You make it in?"

He called me right away and through a raspy, broken voice, said, "Ugh, ya I am. I'm in charge. You actually came in?"

I responded, "Yeah. I just got in. Dude. I'm dying. Did you go home after the party?"

"Naw. I had all my work stuff with me and got an Uber to the airport at four in the morning then slept in the handicap bathroom. I hope you don't mind, I stole a pillow and blanket from your place when I left."

"No sweat, it was probably Gary's. You want me in the checkpoint?"

On the other line a pause took place, indicating either thinking or a hangover so intense momentary brain shutdowns were required to conserve his very few remaining brain cells from working themselves into explosion.

Finally, short of breath, Armando replied, "Naw."

I waited a few seconds to see if that was it. Finally, he concluded with, "Punch-in then go nap. I'll call when I need you."

Smile on face, shoulder tension flung to the floor, I replied, "Alright. Thanks. Can I grab that blanket and pillow from you?"

I napped for a few hours, grabbed a Gatorade and made

my way to the checkpoint to see Armando, hoping there was no work to do. When I arrived, I saw him talking to a passenger, it seemed heated. I approached tentatively. Armando grabbed me and drew me in, signalling I remove my name-tag.

The first words I processed in the conversation were from Armando, spoken like an inmate heading to the basement: condescendingly. "Sir, just because your son is lactose intolerant doesn't mean you need eighteen litres of other liquids for him. I'm pretty sure the plane doesn't even serve milk, it certainly isn't going to rain it from the ceiling."

Outraged, (I assume. He may have been a good actor) the passenger responded, "Do you know who I am you ignoramus?"

I decided it was my turn to join the party and contributed, "That seems irrelevant to the topic, unless of course, you're airport security ... but wait that's us."

The passenger continued, "If you knew who I was, you'd let me take anything I want on this plane," ignoring my comment.

"If you knew who I was you'd let meeee take anything I want on the plane," I countered.

Armando laughed and added, "Who exactly are you sir? He who defies laws."

In typical passenger who is a nobody fashion, he answered, "Oh, you'll find out ... " He paused to look for a name written on our shirts. Mine was pushed so far into my pocket, I was in jeopardy of puncturing my balls; he was hopeless.

"When is it we will find out?" Armando asked.

The passenger's neck jutted out, mimicking a landlord ostrich stretching his lengthy appendage over a tenants shoulder to peek inside the apartment, scoping the scene for drug paraphernalia. This went on for a few seconds, confusing Armando and I, leaving me to wonder what the devil he was doing. Was he looking for a supervisor? Surveying the checkpoint for worms to eat? Stretching his neck mid-conversation for some peculiar reason? Armando and I side-eyed each other quizzically, both curious about his actions.

Finally, the man stopped pelican-ing a trout and answered, "Just as soon as I land, you mall security guard."

Armando quickly countered, "Seems unlikely you're even getting into the air in the first place."

I added, "Especially with three-hundred pounds of fruit drank."

The man was bursting at the seams, his worn-down collar joining suit.

"You two don't know who you are messing with. You sit around here with your minimum wage job, doing nothing; probably go back to your apartments that have cockroaches and your pregnant girlfriends. You're useless little assholes!!"

What an elaborate backstory he'd created for us. Ten points for creativity. Unfortunately for him, in the process he'd managed to pass into very dangerous territory. Where was he failing to gather the clues that we weren't to be trifled with? Mid-gizzard?

Armando cupped his hand over his mouth then signalled for me to do the same. I got the hint: he didn't want the cameras reading our lips.

"You listen, and you listen good sir," he whisper-shouted. "I'm about five seconds away from pressing the alarm and saying you just threatened to kill me and my colleague. I may even throw in that you threatened us with rape, just for a laugh. I have a feeling he'll back me up." He looked over to me for approval. I replied with a head-nod.

"Okay then," he continued. "So you can either leave right now without your month's supply of juice boxes, or you can get dragged out of here by the cops in front of your family. What'll be?"

The passenger's eyes raised in alarm. His creased brow, squinted eyes and pursed mouth, relaxed. Adrenaline relocated from fight to flight. Without another word, he began sprint-stepping away.

"Sir, wait!!"

Apparently, Armando wasn't done.

"I said, what will it be?"

"I'll go, I'll go. Sorry."

He gathered his family and left. Triumphantly, I spiked the juice boxes, one by one into the garbage. Armando went back to his spot in the private search room; the altercation hadn't even fazed him.

# I'M HEAD-OVER-HEELS EXCITED FOR THIS ONE

Alice is a co-worker. My most beautiful co-worker. *Stares into the sky with eyes wide-open, mouth agape and with an overall creepy, lustful disconnect. Our first interaction at work was shocking to her, but less so for me. I approached her and one of our weirdo co-workers while sitting next to each other outside a checkpoint. Tom, the weirdo, was holding a book and the two were talking.

I interrupted to say, "Hey Tom, don't you usually get your mom to read you your books?" then walked away. In the corner of my eye, I caught Alice giggling. I was in love. When we became friends, she mentioned that she didn't know what to say to Tom afterwards because she thought I was being serious, seeing as he's weird and gives off that, 'my mom reads my books for me', vibe. Following the encounter, I'd see Alice here and there, however, I never spoke to her; worried she was a super-hot, sex-cyborg, Trojan-horsed into our team by Big Brother to intimidate confessions of breaches by employees through hotness. Actually, I didn't talk to her because I worried about boners; our work cargos hide them poorly, and her gorgeousness invoked them well.

As I got to know Alice, I realized she was pretty cool; a reality that meant seducing her through acting like someone cool would be futile. So, I gave up on marrying or kidnapping her and having a forced wedding ceremony in which a stuffed dog some moronic ex-lay gave me for a Christmas gift, a cool lamp I found on the side of the road, and my furnace played witnesses to our matrimony. Instead, I became friends with her, hoping she had a slightly less, but similarly, attractive sister with lower standards and a higher threshold for public boners and dating someone who only wants to date you because they think your sister is the hottest person in the world.

On a shift soon after meeting Alice, we were fated by Aphrodite (or directed by the Supervisor) to work the metal detector together. Here's where a better writer describes the weather, surroundings, political turmoil. Locked onto Alice's gaze, I couldn't help but envision our life together: cuddling; more cuddling; stuff that makes you tired and want to get to cuddling after you stop sweating. Knocked from my stupor, I noticed Alice's lips moving; those gorgeous, gorgeous lips ... I was supposed to be answering a question she was in the process of asking. I guessed at it.

"Oh, no, I didn't see him come through. I was ... " I paused from explaining to her why I hadn't been paying attention to think of my reason ... anything other than mentioning the cuddling fantasy would be fine. "I was picturing us cuddling." Doh!! I bashfully laughed. A joke always diverts creepy proclamations, doesn't it? She half-heartedly giggled as well, skeptically squinting before ordering a passenger back. For the next thirty minutes, we stood at the metal detector chatting and sending geologically-tarded passengers back to remove metal.

Here's a brief overview of metal detector etiquette, for those of you wondering if you too are geologically-tarded (in this sense I mean delayed, or slow, retarded as, so yes, it's okay).

Ways you should walk through the metal detector:

1. Hands by your sides.
2. Like you normally walk.

Ways you shouldn't walk through the metal detector:

1. Hands in the air, like you just don't care.
2. In any type of flamboyantly chaotic, spastic flair. (ex. The worm.)

Thirty minutes in, a thirty-year-old-ish girl in corduroys and a flower-print flowy blouse, clearly stolen from Willy Nelson's living room, had her boarding pass scanned and then approached the metal detector. Without hesitation, Hippy Dippy launched forward like a gymnast preparing to spring into her floor routine. Usually, walking is done with feet. She took a different approach. Her hands touched the ground. Her hips rotated and her legs sprang towards the ceiling. This is where the trouble began for her, and humour for us.

First, her left leg smashed the upper part of the machine's frame, inciting violent burst of alarm beeps. Her other leg followed and it too smashed machine. Without forward momentum, her equilibrium became confused and, after momentarily resting on the frame, decided to obey gravity. Beginning in slow motion and then accelerating to a speed demonstrative of a brain's conscious effort to smash the ground as hard as possible —thus guaranteeing a concussion and loss of every memory its moron owner had acquired in life—she head-butted the hard concrete floor with her skull. Not fazed by the connection, she sprang to her feet, smiling and then began walking towards her belongings, somehow unaware that the drunk tumbleweed act didn't comply with metal detector protocol.

My common reaction to nonsense in life is indifference; this occasion was no different. I calmly said to her, "Upside down and inside out, you're not about to show this party what you're all about. Please go back and walk through the metal detector upright. If this concept is foreign to you, refer to your grade ten science book, under the heading Cro-Magnon Man. He mastered the strut."

I turned back to Alice and wrapped the ordeal up by saying, "That is the type of adult that wears those shoes with roller skates built into them." Still keeled over, laughing uncontrollably, she replied, "She so is," through gasps for air. Maybe I could laugh her to the altar? If David Spade bedded Heather Lochlear ...

Not long after the incident, yet another dumb ballsack made the metal detector Hall of Shame while I was working the position. Once again I used the word -tarded, this time, not in the PC way. Sawryyyyy.

I stood alone, leaning against the x-ray machine, confident I was stable enough to structurally remain unsupported; yet, influenced enough by main-stream music and the lyrical stylings of Mo, and DJ's Major Laser to heed caution. I observed a grown man (size-wise) gliding on a scooter, first through the glass partition dividing the checkpoint from the common area, and then as he entered. He climbed off the metal, children's transportation vehicle and began divesting. "This man," I began saying to myself. "Is literally, cruising, for a bruising." I didn't actually think that. My thoughts were filled with all capital letter swears, and a reminder to support whatever politician ran on a pro adult abortion platform next election.

If a scooter can fold up, it's put in a bin and run through the x-ray. If it can't, it's meant to be manually searched. His could not.

*Pause.

Why!!!! is a scooter something that needs to be brought as a carry-on item?? Even for kids. Tell me one good thing that can come from a child (or adult; *sigh) bopping around on the damned contraption? I've never ridden one (OBV), but I imagine they aren't the simplest thing to operate. Plus, who cares if you're a legend at using it? Much like cutting nails on public transportation, I'm sure it can be done, but don't. Why? Why is no one chopping these inconsiderate, disconnected jackasses' heads off with a dull axe? I digress.

Tony Hawk's friendless, poor transportation-choosing brother, put one foot on the scooter and the other on the floor, propelling himself from his divest station. I assumed he'd stop short, then lift it up and ask me what was to be done next, finishing with a, "Cowabunga," or, "Tubular"; like a normal person. I learned my lesson though: no one should ever assume anything regarding adults riding body powered scooters. After gliding through the metal detector and sending the beeps into overdrive, he slid to a stop in front of me, smiling. Smiling!!! Like, ta da!!!

"Seriously?" I asked, calm but suppressing the type of violence microwaves use on corn kernels.

Okay, brace yourself. If you're PC, a millennial, a snowflake of another age, normal, or any number of other people offended by extremely offensive things—please skip ahead to the next paragraph, or smash your Kindle to the floor; any of those methods will work.

I acted on sheer automated reaction. I made a gesture I've used maybe five times since I was ten. Staring the man in his unstable eyes, I opened by mouth, allowing a loud, nasally, "Uhhh," ascend from the back of my throat. I then took my right arm, brought it into the Heil Hitler starting position. Next, I slapped my open right hand off my left chest, hinging at the elbow. Back in my youth, the move is most commonly accompanied by the phrase, "Think hard, retard," on the playground. I felt using the words and the gesture was too much and instead made the motion and then sharply pointed at the other side of the metal detector, then said, "Get the hell off the scooter and go back there, now." He did.

Normally, I'm not so aggro, but I had an excuse. Buried in my pocket at the time, three-quarters of the way finished, rested a book called, *The Coddling of the American Mind*. Essentially, I was nearly through a directive on bitch smacking millennial's sensitive faces until hardened and drained of their baby poop soft sensibilities. So, if you're going to blame anything for my lack of sensitivity, blame literature and libraries.

# DILDOS

Another question I'm often asked about working airport security is whether I see a lot of sex toys. Hell yes I do ... when I'm pulling them outta my bum before I start my shift *wink wink* I kid, I kid. But to answer the question, yes.

I don't actually own a sex toy. I'm not sure what this says about me. If I did, I assume I wouldn't be leaving home with it very frequently. I know for sure that I wouldn't feel a need to travel with it on a business trip or vacation. If only this was the case for everyone else.

Truth be told, my first exposure to sex toys was while babysitting for my neighbour, at the age of twelve. I often crept around the house, opening drawers and cupboards, searching for who knows what. One night, I made my way into the home owner, Louise's, room and opened her nightstand. There sat two items that shocked my church every Sunday, five swear words ever mouthed, mind to the core: One jiggly, purple, fake man hammer and an unrecognizable item.

Bewilderment crossed my face and blood rushed below the elastic band of my grey, Adidas, sweatpants. How appropriate that, in such a creepy-pervert moment, I was wearing creepy, pervert pants. I can tell you now, that the unrecognizable item was anal beads, but at the time I had no idea. I assumed it went in the woman's nether regions, although didn't understand how it could feel good, or the semantics of it at all. I poked at it, shook it, I hate to admit it but I even sniffed it. Next, I gawked at the dildo and pulled out my own throbbing penis to compare them: I was over-matched. I scrolled through the magazines hoping for instructional pictures or some sort of illustration to bring light on the medieval contraption, but couldn't find anything. Eventually, I had to abort project rubber penis and chill out in the kitchen, as time was running dangerously close to Louise's return. I sat there next to a table covered in gigantic bottles of vitamins, dick punching against my whitey tighties, thinking about anything but the past hour, willing my noodle limp.

For weeks afterwards, it perplexed my friends and I; as you may have guessed I told them as soon as humanly possible, until it faded temporarily from my memory. Although, like the first time you hear your parents having sex, I never fully forgot about it. Occasionally, I see a lemonade stirrer or bead necklace that vacuums the image back to my mind, leaving me staring off into space, thinking about the bumpy brain teaser. As kinky as I've gotten, my first exposure to anal beads being that of a fifty-six-year-old, two-hundred and fifty pound woman's, I'll never let the things anywhere near my log snipper.

Nowadays, my exposure to sex toys is usually on an x-ray screen and during bag searches. How often is dependent on how many horn dog degenerates are let out of their sex dungeons and into airport security on any given day. The problem with sex toys is that they are usually made with organics, and indistinguishable organics need to be searched.

The very first dildo I saw at the airport was in a woman's purse, via x-ray image. I immediately created a backstory for her. When she picked up the purse and I was able to put a face to a day-dream, I realized I'd made a horrific mistake. The four-hundred-pound woman dressed in a sweater covered in tiny cartoon cats and leggings, which looked more like sausage casings than pants, was nothing like what I'd fantasized. She had BBQ sauce on her bloody cheek for crying out loud. I could forgive chin or upper lip, but cheek? Why did the feline-friendly tugboat need an emergency orgasm device a hand's reach away for a two-hour flight? I stopped my questioning there, determined to remove the thought from my memory.

Predicting these sex-toy-wielding nymphos based on the image on the x-ray is impossible. A scantily-clad female, with more makeup than Gene Simmons in the cosmetics aisle at Shoppers Drug Mart, is just as likely to pick up a suitcase containing a three-foot vibrator as the four-foot-nine Asian businessman. Much the same with butt plugs, anal beads, vibrators and those always varying dildos.

Fleshlights tend to get searched nearly every time they show up. A fleshlight, for those of you who are normal and don't know, is a fake vagina. The tube shaped item, beaming with glorious, fake vagina organic interior, is almost a dead ringer in composition to an IED. Luckily for recipients, in hand it's more discernible. The first time I sent one for search, I waved over my innocent, religious, female bag-searcher and showed her the area of concern. She plucked it easily from the man's duffle bag. She held it up, then put the cylinder close to her face and examined it. She started twisting it, trying to pry it open. She pulled at the exposed interior.

"Um, are you wondering what it is?" he asked. When she answered yeah, he responded, "It's a sex toy."

She didn't hear him. She was too busy examining it closer, all with her bare hands.

"I use it for personal activities," he continued. She heard this.

"Oh my," she stuttered, nearly dropping it as she did. She shoved it back in the bag while mumbling something incomprehensible under her breath. Presumably something about cutting off her hands later. Before she came back to me, she did the next best thing and bee-lined it for hand sanitizer, bathing herself up to her elbows. She came back as pale as a ghost. Obviously, I laughed, and then smiled; registering the new awesome prank I could pull on co-workers. I've since sent countless dildos, butt plugs, vibrators, and fleshlights for searches, anytime I've gotten lucky and they've graced my x-ray screen.

The funniest thing I've sent has to be a full replica of an ass and vagina. I can't even pretend I didn't know what the image was; it stood out in all its bum cheek and labial glory, just waiting to be intruded on. I called my bag checker (EDT) over and pointed at the item, barely repressing a snicker. Lost in a work stupor, Arianna failed to notice the moulded rump peering back at her. She unzipped the bag. The moment the top was peeled open, her eyes lit up. She simultaneously slammed it down and zipped it back up. She turned to me sharply, and administered a death stare rivalling a zombie's. Neither Arianna nor the passenger said one word to each other. Neither did Arianna or I again for the rest of our shift. Homegirl was pissed.

# DRY AND WILD

While we're on the topic of sex toys …

One day, I was talking to a few co-workers about passengers they'd dealt with that shift. One made typical complaints about an entitled woman not understanding why she wasn't allowed to bring an eighteen-litre bottle of peanut butter on the plane; nothing special. The adorable Alice had a great story. She began with, "I had a passenger come through today that wouldn't stop fighting me about taking his lube."

I settled in, lube stories are usually good.

"Go on," I pushed.

"I took it out of his bag and told him it was too big. He said he needed it badly."

I deliberated, quenching my face in contemplation. "Ugh, maybe I don't actually want to hear this story. I'm trying to limit my exposure to old men applying spermicidal lube."

"He wasn't old," she corrected.

Shocked, fork in an electrical socket, I asked, "How old?"

"Fortyish."

I nodded, taking in a conversation that forced me to picture forty-year-old men applying lubrication to their penises. Oh, airport life, and the mind of an imbecile. That didn't stop my extensive strange men lube application thoughts to interfere with me offering, "He should be able to produce his own dink lube at that age, I think. I don't have extensive research, but I'm still going strong at thirty-five."

Indifferently, she responded, "Yeah, I guess. So, he keeps making a fuss about the lube, holding it up to the light and saying stuff like 'I need my lube. I don't know what I'll do without it.'"

"That's hilarious," I said without laughing, caught up in the sick, twisted images Alice had forced on me. For some reason, I asked, "Don't they sell KY where he was going?" as if, for some reason, feeling bad for the confiscation, she'd Googled pharmacies and their inventory in his final destination to help the guy out.

A 'What are you even asking me?' look crossed her face.

She responded, "Who knows? Then he starts shouting over to his girlfriend, "THEY'RE TRYING TO STEAL MY LUBE, BABE!" There's a crowd of people waiting for their bags, listening. It was super embarrassing."

I pictured the type of man who yells about losing his 150 ml bottle of penis lube across an airport checkpoint. He definitely had exposed chest hair. For sure a tacky, flamboyant dress shirt with sleeves rolled halfway up his forearms. No doubt about it, he wore at least one gold chain. Probably losing his hair but holding on for dear life with a nice little comb-over. Alice is little, cute and generally shy about dramatic passengers, although she will lash out when provoked, much like a baby cheetah.

"What happened next?" I asked. "I'm hooked."

She responded, "I gave him his options, and then he told me there was no way he was throwing it out. By then I was just over it."

I interrupted to say, "He sounds proud of his dry-dick sitch."

"He was obnoxious. Anyways, I took it up to the front, held it up and yelled 'SIR IF YOU WANT TO KEEP YOUR LUBE YOU HAVE TO COME UP HERE AND DUMP HALF OF IT OUT!!'"

Steepling my fingers in devious bad guy fashion, I creepily said, "Wonderful, wonderful! And did he come do it?"

"Nope. I left it there and he never came and did it."

"All that hoopla over his slip and slide juice and he just left it. My goodness. The nerve."

"Yep," she replied. "The lube is probably still sitting there."

"Why'd you tell me that part? Are you assuming I'll go grab it?"

She smirked then answered, "I wouldn't put it past you."

With that, we finished our conversation and I began writing it. Even though to us he was just another weird, irate passenger being dramatic over a dollop of spermicidal lube, I hope for some it may be a life lesson. That life lesson being ... um ... don't buy your lube in industrial size ... I guess.

A few months later, Alice recounted yet another lube story to me, prefacing it with, "I've had a lot of weird lube things happen to me."

I couldn't help but respond with a sexual innuendo riddled, "Yeah you do." Followed by an exaggerated wink. With pen in hand, I requested, "Tell me everything. Spare no detail." I concluded with the unnecessary warning, "You know I'm gonna post this on my blog if it's good, right?" She nodded, a point noted on paper with a time stamp for court, if needed.

She began telling the story by whispering, "He had no shame. He told me he needed his lube as if it was an everyday conversation," from the side of her mouth, wisely leaving out penis-moistening-aid giveaway words in front of the passenger whose bag she was searching.

He left.

She continued. "I pulled out the bottle and discreetly told him it was too large, shielding it with his bag so other people wouldn't see. He reached out and asked if he could look, so I handed it over. He held it up to check how full it was and said he thought there wasn't over 3oz."

I interrupted to ask, "Flaunting it eh?"

"Yes buddy. Thanks for your contribution. So we argued a bit about the size and he kept saying you can't take my lube, I need it. What will I do without it?"

I interrupted again. "How old was he?" Apparently, I have some infatuation with lubers' age. I'd be like those age and weight guessing carnies at the fair if ever left at an oil and lube mechanics. That line was both long and unfunny.

"Forty-ish," she replied. She continued, "He was speaking in a normal voice and everyone could hear him. I was so shocked. He didn't have any shame about it. Like, yeah, I use lube, and yeah, I don't care." I contributed, "I always hide it like you did and say things quietly. They are always just happy for me to throw it away quickly and get the whole thing over with."

Her head involuntarily bobbed in agreement as she said, "Yeah, same, but he really didn't care. So then he says, 'What will I do before my flight?' I was shocked and just laughed and said, I'm sure you'll be fine."

I interrupted again-again. "Let me stop you there. He said what will he do before his flight without lube?"

"Yes," she casually replied. It should be noted that most of Alice's replies to me are done with this air suggesting she's confused as to why I'm once again interrupting her, especially when

I use questions where the answers in whatever she just said.

I asked, "Huh. Is that a thing? People wanking off before flights? If I Google, Tips for dealing with flying anxiety, that'll come up? When I'm peeing during breaks, is someone in a stall five-feet away having at 'er? Is that not pee on the floor?"

Alice laughed and said, "I don't know. Maybe."

I thought for a second, then said, "This reminds me of something an ex, I assumed was crazy, once told me. She'd just gotten back from the beach and I asked how it was. She responded that it was good, but that a female on a towel not far from her had her boyfriend go down on her. Obviously, I was shocked which threw her off. She said people do that all the time, making me think that in all the times I've gone to the beach, I'm somehow missing men filling their pie-holes with minge and sand. Now I'm wondering if there is actually a whole world of sex-craved maniacs just fellating each other nimbly-bimbly every which where."

Finishing the conversation off, Alice casually responded, "Maybe," bored with the conversation and overall unimpressed with my constant tangents which often contain more beach head than Jaw's local.

# IF YOU THOUGHT J-LO'S ASS WAS FAKE …

What's that? Tell you another story about genital moulds? You got it.

My friend Mike walked over to me laughing, in that way you do when you're shocked and can't really think of any other way to react.

"Wat up?" I asked.

Through chuckles, he replied, "You may not believe it."

"I believe everything. I grew up in a religious household."

He laughed, saying, "Fair enough," through the giggles. "I just searched this gross white guy's bag. He was so dried and flaky I covered my mouth and nose the whole search to avoid inhaling his skin." I interrupted with a gem. "When he's cold, they're frosted flakes." He didn't laugh, or seem to notice; just stood quietly—likely internally angry I'd interrupted him with something so stupid.

I urged, "Like the cereal. Get it?"

"Right," he responded.

He continued, "So anyways, I pulled open his stinky duffel bag and sitting there was a fake ass, vagina and all. I quickly zipped the bag back up and said 'Thank you sir, have a nice day'. I hoped to walk away and puke but he decided to explain."

"My wife always makes me bring this on vacation with me, so she knows I won't cheat."

Unperturbed, Mike responded, "That's great sir. You don't need to explain it to me though."

The man continued. "Yeah, it makes her feel a lot better." He paused to figure out what words were socially acceptable when speaking about banging a prosthetic vagina and bum. Finally, he added the unnecessary aside, "Knowing I'm only doing stuff with this. Safer than a prostitute too."

"That's when I threw my arms up in surrender and walked away," Mike explained to me.

I asked, "So the two of you didn't have a threesome with the fake ass and gina then?"

Practically puking on my face, he replied, "Ummm, no."

"Oh, I assumed that was where this story was going."

Mike concluded the conversation with, "You're an idiot."

# LATE ARRIVAL

I have a few friends who work as EMS workers in the area around the airport. They're good paramedics. I, would not be. They deal with so much crap. Sometimes it's literally crap. Adult, human, crap, and not in the toilets. There's a single, older, wealthy lady living within their region who makes up roughly fifty percent of the calls they receive.

Ol' Yeller, calls over sore throats (inner, outer, doesn't matter); gas (butt, natural, doesn't matter); and most commonly, indigestion. Congregated outside of Barb's house, police, fire and EMS, often discuss ways to cut her phone lines, or windpipe, while one unlucky, rookie paramedic goes through the necessary precautionary checkup. Usually, the night ends with someone scolding, "Barb, stop eating cheese. You know it upsets your stomach," as if she's a lactose-intolerant goldfish. If I was cruising around at four in the morning, half way through a twelve-hour shift, drinking my tenth cup of coffee just to stay awake, and fresh from a call where I pulled a baby out of a screaming, procrastinating woman, I'd ignore any call to Barbs. At best, I'd pretend I was going, but take a quick nap on the side of the road, leaving the twat to fart away with only her lonesome thoughts and stinky furniture.

As one can imagine, it's fun to compare stories with my EMS friends. Even more fun is discussing calls they get to the airport—ones I can learn intimate details about and woo the co-workers who are discussing it with missing information.

My airport employs around forty-thousand people and a lot of my friends' calls are for airport staff. These are even more fun to hear about. My paramedic friends aren't supposed to tell me who the calls are for, but hint enough to make me go, "Ohh-hhh, I think I know who that is." They even know a few of my co-workers by name. One guy who I work with rings 911 so often that he knows a lot of the paramedics' names. They have a nick-name for him. Not an enduring one as you can probably guess. I can't really write it without giving the person away to people who know him. I will, however, tell a story that illustrates pretty well what kind of guy he is.

After moving out of the apartment uptown with Gary, I got a place more downtown. The location allowed me to ditch my ever-problematic car, exchanging it for public transit, more reading time and some insight into what a Gary Busey reality show might be like. A few weeks after purchasing my first monthly metro-pass, I jumped on the subway, heading for work. Ten minutes into the journey, the train came to an abrupt halt, mid-stop. An announcement rang out, "An emergency alarm has been pressed. This train will be delayed until an emergency response crew arrives on the scene." The full subway car of commuters collectively sighed with annoyance. An hour later the problem was resolved.

I got to my work locker, slammed it open and threw my jacket inside. A co-worker standing nearby asked, "Why are your panties in a knot?" Before I answered, another co-worker burst into the room, obviously late as well. He started slamming things harder than me. I turned my attention to him, annoyed he was stealing my anger-thunder.

"What's wrong with you?" I asked.

"Don't even ask," he spat in my direction.

Before I had a chance to accept the comment as my turn to start speaking again, he went off. "I pressed the emergency strip on the subway because I thought I might be having a panic attack over being underground. It took the paramedics thirty minutes to get there. I was so annoyed sitting there waiting. Last time I pushed it they were way faster."

Outraged, enraged, ragin-cajuned, I spat, "I'm sorry. You pressed the emergency strip because you thought you *may* be having a panic attack? What kinda sense does that make? There's literally one minute between stops. How in hell did you think the paramedics would get to the subway from their station, run through pitch black tunnels a few miles, then find you inside one of fifteen subway cars, quicker than you just getting off thirty seconds later and walking outside?"

I was fuming. This wasn't my first run-in with the co-worker. He's a constant pain in everybody's ass. As one of his minor daily discretions, he's well known for walking off the line because, "I'm just not feeling it," leaving everyone to pick up his slack. He was shocked by my anger.

"Why do you even care what I do? Why should I get off the subway? I pay taxes!!"

The comment wasn't out of character for him. I've heard him claim he has the right to do just about everything, including spitting cherry seeds on the ground of our work lunchroom, because he pays taxes. I replied, "So do the hundred and fifty other people on the train. Now they have less money to do so, because you made them late for work."

His annoying face scrunched to within inches of collapsing in on itself. It sprung back and went taut and red, he was about to sprout an extra alien set of teeth and bite my head off.

He threw down his bag and jacket then started walking in my direction. I braced myself for a fight. Instead, he rushed past, and then stopped at the door. He turned back towards me and spat, "I'm going to tell on you," before leaving. My last thought as he raced away was, "Why didn't he use all that speed and determination to walk his dumb ass off the subway, instead of pushing the strip and making me late?" Also, tell on me? Now that's funny.

# PULP NON-FICTION

"It happened again," I declared, throwing my arms up in surrender. Riffling through his locker next to me, Armando squinted quizzically in my direction for ten seconds, and then responded, "Herpes?"

Feigning outrage, I spat, "What? No. I've never had herpes." I tucked my chin into my chest and whispered, "That you know of."

With herpes off the table, Armando deflated. Gumpshunless, he asked, "I give up then. What happened again?"

"Madness, Armando. Madness on the subway."

As he placed the last of his uniform insignia onto his shirt, Armando responded, "Sounds like the title to a really bad action movie."

"This isn't a movie, it's the real life of anyone who has to take that gosh darned underground, motorized worm every day. The crazies I grew up with were harmless, sitting in broken

lawn chairs, watering used tires on their front yard, and screaming, 'When's Judith coming by for Scrabble at the top of their
lungs.'"

"Ah, the good ol' days," Armando contributed.

He asked, "What happened this time?"

"Someone had an appetite for ink and destruction."

He contributed, "I'm intrigued," while liberating bar-
nacles from his booger cave.

"Go on," he suggested. So I did, because I'm a pleaser.

"Armando, at the airport we deal with freaks, psycho-
paths and would-be terrorist, but honestly, sometimes the subway is worse. This is what happened."

I recited my tale:

"Give me your book!" It was ten in the morning, much
too early for a book mugging. I was confused. I lifted my eyes
from a softcover copy of Philip Roth's, *The Human Stain*, perplexed. The man, looming imposingly, albeit a tad wobbly, was
exuding alcohol and stink, stink lines. Dressed in stained, drab
clothes, the five-foot-five leathery man in my personal space
was exactly the type of person I tried to avoid on public transit, *by* reading. Yet there he stood, demanding my shield, for his
own.

"I'd rather not give it to you," I delivered, maintaining
reasonableness that was a tad stoic, given the situation. This
situation, contrasted to an ideal subway setting, gained the attention of nearly all thirty members of our car—we had an audience. I wouldn't be stifled though, I was newly emerged in the
world of spirituality and meditation. Time to put that hokey-
pokey bologna to use.

"Give it to me," he slurred. Despite the conflict, neither
the book thief nor I were willing to raise our voices, both of us in
control of ourselves. Although, judging by his stink, he wasn't in
complete control of his bowels.

"I honestly would just rather not give you the book." A logical response, I thought.

He retaliated, "But I want it." A childish response, I thought, except as a response by children; then, it would be just a response. I wondered if he'd shifted his approach for getting my book from aggression to pity.

"Like I mentioned earlier, I'd just rather not give it to you, I'm reading it. What do you want with it anyway?" The bystanders on the train started watching more blatantly, less subtle with their listening as they became more comfortable, presumably because of my soothing, Buddhist tone. If they are anything like me, they hoped for an aggressive exchange they could chat about later by the office water cooler.

"To eat it," he sincerely replied.

As I responded, "Now you're definitely not getting it. I think you can understand why I don't want you eating my book," I shook my head in disappointment, letting him know through neck swivelling he'd let me down.

He was unperturbed. "I'd let you eat my book," he offered with a straight, genuine face. If nothing else, he was generous.

"It's okay. I have my own book to eat, but thanks."

"Please?" he persisted.

I was on my last rope, rolling my eyes, shaking my head in disbelief, even thinking mean thoughts about him. I responded, "No, really, I'm not giving it to you."

"Yes," he spat.

"No," I stoically recited.

With that, he ripped the book from my hands and, spine towards me, bit down, putting his human stain on my copy of *The Human Stain.*

"Well, now you can have it, buddy," I sedately recited. My tone took on a smidgen of the weight of my irritation; I don't know how Gandhi did it. I uncrossed my legs, sighed and sat up straight, attempting to show my displeasure through posture. Also to protect me, should he decide to add meat to his lunch. Demonstrating a new sense of sanity, the aggressor snapped out of his drunken book biting stupor and apologetically pushed the book back at me.

"I don't want it anymore, you bit it," I explained.

"I don't want it either."

"You claimed it by biting it. It's yours now pal."

"Next stop, Jane, Jane station," rang out through the train by an automated recording. Five seconds later, after a good old-fashioned stare off, the book bandit dropped the slobbered, teeth indented book back into my lap and then casually walked through the subway car doors. For a dramatic exit, he made a curtain call. As the subway fired up again and slowly edged forward, the book bandit turned and locked eyes with me through the window. He placed a finger to his left nostril and blew a snot rocket to the ground, holding eye contact with me until a tunnel blocked our way. Eating my book had apparently clogged up his nose.

I finished the story as Armando and I entered the checkpoint. I turned to him and asked, "So what do you think?"

"Think? Think? Buddy, it isn't what I think, it's what I know. What I know is that my Beemer goes 150 swiftly, and that the only weirdo in it is you, when I give you rides. Buy another car. Now, I can see you're out of sorts, and in no position to be working, therefore, I recommend we punch in then disappear; chillin until you get yourself together and get over that book of yours."

I nodded. With that we punched in and then left the checkpoint, returning a few hours later complaining of diarrhea.

# DIARRHEA

Diarrhea, my, nearly-foolproof, get-out-of work-related problem/made up excuse. It springs up a ton during sports' playoffs. Most basketball playoff games I get it around halftime and it almost always gets worse through the fourth quarter and OT. My tummy's usually okay for baseball, but it tends to act up around the eighth inning of World Series games, the rumble beginning in about the seventh. Similar timing disturbs my tumultuous gut during World Cup of soccer shootouts, NHL late thirds and NFL ... Actually, it's so bad on Sundays, I just pre-emptively book-off. Leave that jet poop sitch for at home.

I assume it's coincidence, but any time close friends or family are flying through my port of air, my belly rumbles to life, growling me out of the checkpoint, only to settle down at the exact moment they need help pushing through a long line to the front of Nexus.

On my Fridays, when friends start texting and snapping

pics and videos of them drinking and doing fun stuff, there it is, that ol chestnut, potential poopy pants reporting for unwanted doody (play on words, supposed to be duty. Killin it!!!). The acting training I picked up from my church's rendition of the nativity comes in handy.

"Supervisor, I need to use the washroom. I don't feel well."

Fast forward twenty minutes. I return.

"It didn't go too, too well in there sir. I'm unfortunately going to have to head home on account of a bad case of the diarrhea."

And off I go, the colitis version of Keyser Soze, butt-clenching shuffle walk until I'm out of the supervisor's sight, then a bold, brisk jaunt full throttle to the bus.

# THE SUBWAY
# MANAGER

Not long after I was involuntarily a guest at the book bandit's feast, I once again ran into subway laughs on my way to work. This time, at least I had a friend to share the experience with. Maybe I should buy a helicopter, I worry the lunacy will rub off on me.

So there we are, me and Antonia, sitting on the subway exchanging horror stories—her three days in, me a seasoned veteran—when on walks a blonde, Cabbage Patch Doll-looking fella. I can sense the subway's momentum switch from sane to something else; something unpredictable and subway-like. I continued talking to Antonia, but kept the guy in my peripheral; he was wearing tear-aways, something was going down for sure. He started muttering. He frantically looked around. His head darted too rapidly to take anything in; yet, he seemed concerned. He grabbed at the tear-aways. Please God, let him pull off those snap-up pants, please, please, Magic Mike it up, pal.

"I'm the best manager around," he shouted.

Yes, you are fella. Yes, you are. Let the world know it. He gained everyone's attention. Who doesn't want to hear what the best manager around has to say? He burst out with another fantastic declaration, "I've got them all in my back pocket." Probably not, since your pants are sporty and back pocketless, but I like where you are heading with this Mark Cuban, preaching to the choir.

He reiterated, "The best manager around." Alright, you're losing momentum here homeboy, shift it down a gear and get back on track.

"I'm the strongest guy on here, look at me! Look at me!" Crap, this isn't the direction you want a coocoo for Cocoa Puffs taking. What happened to the business discussion? Who's going to take a manager with so little focus seriously? Okay good, you're standing up. There's no better way to address the masses, heading to work on a Tuesday morning, than by showing your dominant position standing.

Oh yes! He ripped his shirt like Hulk Hogan, right down the centre; a real boss move. What a professional. Starting from the collar, gripping with both hands and pulling down, all with his managerial strength, he made short work of the flimsy cotton. He nearly tore all the way through, but paused for dramatic effect.

"I'm the best manager!!" he declared again in a fantastical burst of scream, drifting through the word manager as he finished off the cheap fabric holding together his *Oakland Automart* T-shirt. His proclamation advanced from best manager around; he's now the best manager, plain and simple. The cold air on his nipples and navel brought on a chilled demeanour. He sat passive and belly out. Two stops later, he sauntered off the cart. The subway, no place for him, not with a company to run.

When Antonia and I arrived at work forty-minutes later, she was still in shock.

"Buddy, do you think he's still out there with a ripped shirt?"

"Honestly," I contemplated. "I'm sure his assistant or secretary had a fresh top waiting for him."

Pushing through fits of laughing hysteria, Antonia urged, "Stop!! Seriously!!"

"Seriously? What's serious about this situation? He was wearing tear-aways, I'm sure he can handle a little bit of breeze."

We entered the checkpoint, punched in and joined Armando at the supervisor's podium.

"Antonia," I began. "Tell Armando all about our subway ride."

She smiled and opened her mouth, obviously excited to tell him.

"Enoughhhhhhh," he cried. "Enough about the damned public transit. I'm not poor. I don't want to hear about those miscreants and the filthy things they participate in on that weird sex tube."

He looked poised to continue but I interjected in a childish voice to say, "You have a weird sex tube." That was the end of that.

# EMERGENCY
# EMERGENCY

I stumbled from the bar. Nearly tripped over a curb; barely dodged a shaky parked car. Halfway through a parkette, I remembered I had to work four hours later, at 6 a.m. I pulled out my phone, dropped it. Picked it up and started scrolling through numbers for the book-off line. I dropped it again. Somehow, in the time between dropping the phone and picking it up again, I forgot I'd called the number.

"Hello? Who's this?" I asked.

The caller (?) on the other end sighed, clearly aware I was drunk or using a phone for the first time.

"You called me," he explained. "This is the airport security book-off line."

I laughed, possibly out of confusion, then hung-up. I stomped into my house a few minutes later. At the door, I ripped off my jacket. By the couch, I was topless and working on my belt. I smashed into the bathroom wall while removing my pants, failing to realize my pant leg was tucked into my sock. My phone crashed to the floor. It had been dropped more times than molly at The Weeknd's house. The crash reminded me that I needed to book-off work.

*Repeat my previous efforts to make it happen.

I heard, "Hello, book-off. How can I help you?" through the first waves of my pee. Through the waterfall sounding reverberation of urine hitting porcelain, I explained I needed the next day, Thursday, off for religious reasons.

"Which ones?" he asked. He caught me off guard and, with my dick out, I might add.

"Um," I stuttered. "The usual ones."

He sighed again, and then went on asking my details to book me off. It was my first attempt. Surprisingly, it hasn't been my worst.

The process is supposed to go more-or-less how I described, minus the drunk interludes. A third party company records the booking-off employee's information and the reason they give. They then report it to our employer. What I didn't know until too late, is that the recording is thorough, including the number I've called from, right down to how I sounded during the call.

Even now that I know the calls are recorded, I sometimes drunk-forget and make outlandish book-offs. A manager approached me the day after I'd booked off. We had been at a co-worker's wedding together the night before. He skeptically assessed me. He asked, "You were at the same wedding as me Saturday night, yeah?"

"Of course I was, Dan. We shared that magical kiss at midnight. Right before you ran away and left your glass slipper behind. How could I forget?"

Skeptical face posturing further, he responded, "Rightttttt. What I find a tad bit odd is the record log says you booked off for an emergency ... emergency. What exactly is an emergency emergency? Is one a noun and the other a verb?"

"That's an obvious one, Dan." I took my time with a slow sip of my Gatorade, the reptilian assistant purchased for re-hydrating depleted electrolytes from the night before. Even I was stumped by my idiotic book-off excuse, but I wasn't going to let that dissuade or skip me up. Convinced I had at least a somewhat believable lie, I explained, "An emergency, necessitated by another emergency. Duh!!"

Unconvinced, Dan asked, "How does Tim's wedding qualify as a double emergency?"

I shook my head in disbelief. I further explained my book-off. "Not a double emergency. You aren't getting it. An emergency, emergency. Get it straight. The answer is quite simple. The first emergency is Tim getting married. As you know, I'm never pleased when my friends leave me for a woman. Remember my whole one vagina for the rest of your life theory? Anyways, the second emergency is me forgetting to get someone to take my shift. I was obviously not going to pass up an open bar and steak to go to work. Duh!!"

"Neither are an emergency," he calmly (and arrogantly I might add) stated.

I childishly replied, "To youuuuu."

He asked, "When did you book off? I was with you all day and night."

"Yeah, you were big guy," I took a brief pause from sucking back Gator jizz to motion a high-five. He left me hanging. "I'll be honest with you, Dan, I may have called shortly after dessert, a few minutes after those shots."

"That was way after your shift had started, and you were wasted at the time."

I 'Tsk Tsk' head nodded, while explaining, "Dan, if I call sober they think it's an imposter calling for me. It's inconceivable to them I'd be booking off sober, on a Saturday, and for a real reason. Really Dan, sometimes I feel you don't even know me."

Later that day, Armando sauntered up to me grinning. I was searching bags, in the midst of a classic game of, "No you can't bring it." "Yes I can bring it," game with a passenger unwilling to give up his "80$" hair gel. I lost my sympathy for hair maintenance about the same time genetics encouraged me towards spending more on Bic Razors and hats than shampoo and combs, the results evident in my unemphatic, indifferent stare that was level with the man's left shoulder.

"I'd like to proposition you," Armando declared.

I replied, "Buy me a pint and I'm all yours." The passenger briefly paused from his tirade on brand loyalty, a rant provoked by my advice of, "Why don't you buy another one when you land?"

He and Armando fired up again at the same time, my attention shifted to my co-worker.

"I heard about your book-off reason. Brilliant man, just brilliant. What's more serious than an emergency emergency? Who's gonna question that?" I opened my mouth to Mel Lastman a Bad Boy worthy rendition of, "NOOOOO BODYYYY," but he shushed me, nearly shoving his outstretched index and F-U digit into my mouth.

He continued, "The answer my friend, is NOOOO BODYYYY." You son of a beehive, I thought. Stealing my over-used, dumb commercial line.

"I'm not here to suck your horn over your book-off though. Nawwww, I've got bigger plans. Ideas brother. Ideas." That's where he stopped talking and walked away, leaving bad hair guy and me standing speechless, wondering what the buck had just happened.

I caught up to Armando a few hours later in the lounge. I began by asking, "Care to elaborate about your ideas?" He looked at me like a previously lost, rescued moron: dumb-founded.

"You came up to me, went on about my book-off; said you had ideas, then left. Ring any bells?"

"Ahh, yes. I've got a proposition for you about that," he recalled.

Shaking my head in frustration, I responded, "We've been over that."

He went on. "How about you and I see who can do the funnier book-off?"

*A reasonable person's response: "No."

*My response: "Okay. I'll book off tomorrow and win."

Deviously chuckling a villain- worthy laugh, Armando countered, "No, I'll book off tomorrow and win."

"You are something else," I concluded.


Two days later:

Armando, apparently sporting his default facial expression, grinned while asking, "Run into any dinosaurs lately?"

I hadn't, from what I remembered, but decided to indulge his fantastical question.

"Of course I have. F-ing T-Rex got into my garden again. Tore my cabbage to shreds. I had to have impromptu coleslaw for dinner. Wish those damn beasts would go extinct already."

He looked at me perplexed. He asked, "What are you talking about?"

I mimicked his befuddlement.

I asked, "What are youuuuu talking about?"

He took a deep breath, hoping patience clings to oxygen molecules.

"Your reason for booking off yesterday. You don't remember?"

Pursing my mouth, squinting my eyes, and tilting my head ever so slightly, I responded, "Refresh my memory. That damn T-Rex has flustered me to no ends. I can't remember a dang thing."

'Ahhhhhhhhh' burned in his eyes as he explained, "For our competition, you booked off because of dinosaurs."

Time to spark the Ah's further. "Doesn't ring any bells. When was this?"

Lava threatened to roll down his cheeks. "Yesterday, late. Stop being a moron."

"Hmmmm," I contemplated. "I remember being at the bar. I had a couple wobbly pops, and then...," I paused. I held my index finger in the air like a genius from a cartoon coming to a profound realization. I announced, "Voila!!! It's all coming back to me now."

Armando shook his head and walked away. His final comment was astute and accurate. "You're an idiot!!" he declared.

I pried him throughout the day, attempting to flush out his book-off. I couldn't though; the prideful silver medallist retained a sealed vault, blubber and a slippery bod, protecting his failed jump attempt.

# DICKS OUT, FOR THE BOYS. DICKS OUT FOR THE BOYS

W ithout warning, I opened WhatsApp to an unloaded video of a naked man. My friend Alex had recorded it during his break and then, for some reason, immediately sent it to me. I watched all thirty-seven seconds, including the last ten, the dick heavy portion of the film. If you focused on only the naked man's face, you'd assume he was out for a casual stroll. Luckily, he wasn't, because the nippy winter weather would have shrunk an already lacking appendage, leaving the star of Alex's movie nearly invisible. I won't rip on the Emperor's New Cloak too badly; he's clearly unwell. I messaged Alex back, "Nice dick," then forwarded the video to a few friends.

Surprisingly, the airport is no stranger to nudity. The first time I saw someone naked at the facility for harbouring 02 was late at night. I'd just closed a checkpoint with Armando and the two of us were sitting on passenger benches in an empty hallway, wasting time.

"What did you steal today?" I asked him.

He looked up at the ceiling, checking for cameras above us. Nada. He reached into both pockets and pulled out his haul.

"Pretty good score of loot," he announced.

He dropped a few memory sticks, some jewellery, a couple a Fit-bits, and money onto my lap. "Behold, my retirement fund."

Down the hall, barely visible, a man stood wobbling in dimmed light. His unstable stance drew our attention. He moved closer, to within about fifty-feet.

"Are you thinking what I'm thinking?" Armando asked.

I offered, "That this lighting is setting the perfect mood for a good ol' make-out session and we should invite that guy to join?"

"Ew, what? No. Why would I think that?"

"Yeah, Yeah. Me either," I stuttered, pretending I was pretending to not be serious. "Um, just joking. What were you thinking?"

Unperturbed by my nonsense, Armando picked up where he'd left off. "That guy is going to do something crazy."

"No doubt about it. Look how sketchy he's acting," I agreed.

Our predictions quickly came true. First, the man took off his sweater and spiked it to the ground with football touchdown, celebratory zeal, proving us right.

I screamed, "Take it off!!" loud enough that the words could reach him and titillate his psycho eardrums. He heard and looked our way. In unison, Armando and I chanted, "Take it off!! Take it off!!" He obliged. Next to go was his T-shirt, leaving us with a view of his nips. We continued to chant—our interest had been peaked. He undid his belt. It was getting too real. Man-tits I could live with seeing, a cack was out of the question. We stopped chanting and pretended the stripper no longer existed, going back to Armando's jewels. Magic Mike wasn't dissuaded and tugged down his pants, leaving only boxer briefs on, clearly bought by a grandma or aunt. Our attempts to ignore him were futile; no one can resist looking at an almost naked stranger in public.

"What should we do?" Armando asked.

I lulled the question over for a second, quickly coming up with the perfect solution. I proclaimed, "Find a place to get one dollar bills quickly so he doesn't feel like we don't appreciate the show. I'm'ma make it rain up in this bitch."

Through confused squints, Armando explained, "I meant more like should we call the police?"

My face lit up, we were on the same page. I expanded his idea with, "Oh, good idea. Make this strip show themed."

Our entertainment was ready for the grand finale, no time to wait for his backup dancers. Boom goes the dynamite, dick out for the boys!! Down the hall, nude guy yanked what was left of his hidden skin from its oppressor.

"Well," I said to Armando. "This just got weird."

I thought we were his audience, the lucky recipients of his entertainment, but I was wrong. He turned to face a large glass window, taking in the runway. Twenty minutes later, he was still in the same position, frozen as if a real life David. Armando and I had to leave, although for obvious reasons were hesitant to get any closer to the nude dude. He continued standing against the glass, his poor penis wondering where the heck his best friend Calvin Klein had gone.

Unfortunately, the only way to the locker room was to

traverse dangerously close to the nudist's exposed genitals. The hallway is about fifty-feet wide. It has a few bathrooms and water fountains on one side and the huge window wall that Dick Out was against, on the other. Armando and I tucked tightly to the wall, insinuating that deviation of more than a couple inches would plunge us into an abyss. I guess the alternative was actually even worse than that, the potential to touch or be touched by a flaccid wiener. The water fountains protrude from the wall a bit, leaving us the option of moving a few feet closer to scrotum or ducking under or climbing over them, remaining pinned to the wall. There was no way I was risking dick, so ducked under, barely squeezing through the tight space. Armando went around, leaving himself vulnerable, a move that left me to believe he wanted some action.

If ... and this is a very big if, the man was sane, Armando and I probably looked like a complete bunch of lunatics to him. That obviously wasn't the case though, so I advance the plot. We got past, turned the corner and quick-walked away, keeping an eye over our shoulders, being cautious he wasn't following. We walked over to a police kiosk and spoke to the first person we saw.

"Officer, there's a man standing around the corner with his dick and balls out."

"And?" he asked.

I was shocked by the response. I'd expected him to spring into action, drawing his gun, ready to snipe the man's undercarriage off.

"And ... nothing I guess," I said before shrugging. I then prompted Armando to walk away with me, and that's that. The end. That guy is probably still on the prowl, naked, in some hidden recess of the airport.

# THOSE ARE BOMB ASS BERKS

Out of some sick, twisted joke by fate, I work with this ding-dong named Peter all the time. Other co-workers, I'll only see every few months or longer, because of different checkpoints or start times. This bell-end, I see almost daily. If he was just your standard moron, I wouldn't mention him, mostly because I hate thinking of the guy, but he's not. He's acidic. Idiotic to a fault.

Peter is an imbecile. He's even got that imbecile shell, a body constantly defying motions beneficial to efficiency or making people like you. His head involuntarily swivels. His brain can only do so much and instead of providing instructions to his neck to stay sturdy, it conserves his limited brain cells for commanding things he'd otherwise forget to do, such as assisted breathing, reminders to make his heart beat, and apparently to laugh in my least favourite way. In a movie of his life —which would never be made unless someone framed him for a murder they'd committed (he's too stupid to perform all the lucid steps required in a murder detailed enough to make it to media, other than an episode of World's Dumbest Criminals)— his head and body would be played by Peter Griffin (which is why I've named him Peter for this story), the slovenly character from Family Guy and his facial hair by a 1960's pubic bush.

However, Peter's most distinguishable feature is not his resemblance to obese cartoon characters and pubic hairstyle choice. No, that's just the tip of the iceberg. His laugh is a guttural A-A-A-A-A spasm, gritty like an old, rusty chainsaw firing up, escaping his donut-hole-shaped mouth, slowly, willing its way from the Cheetos and Mars bars lining his bathtub-shaped stomach. If you can't think of the noise, imagine if Monty Burns from the Simpsons and Bevis and Butthead banged one out in the strangest cartoon three-way ever and produced a baby (yes, this is possible in cartoon world). That inbred, freak of nature laughs and—there you have it.

A few days ago, Peter was doing ETD. He pulled a bin from the search rollers, laboriously carried it to his work station and scanned it. The image showed only a pair of thin, rubber sandals, one maybe a little slightly denser than the other, probably a slight defect in production, a lesser version of Peter's large production defect. The sandal had either been sent because of the discrepancy or because someone was screwing around in the x-ray room. I'd have cleared it and let it go, apologizing to some barefoot (or if it was a German person, the thick-socked, cargo pant with the zipper to change them into shorts-wearing individual) passenger for wasting their time. Peter picked up the left sandal and held it towards the light, scrutinizing it with an intensity that suggested either the light helped penetrate the rubber or that he had x-ray vision. The light was thirty feet away and dim and his eye sight resembles a newborn hamster, meaning his scrutinizing was for show; a show only he was involved in, thank goodness. His only real superpower is diabetes and an ability to eat a full vending machine worth of treats in one sitting—who was the guy kidding?

"I'm afraid this looks a little bit off," he said to the passenger, pausing at the end to do his Butthead/Bevis/Burns laugh. The passenger didn't think it was funny and asked, "What do you mean? It's just a sandal."

I had to hand it to the passenger, it was just a sandal. A normal, run of the mill, non-bomb, sandal. Peter didn't think so.

"Yeah, but you can see in my image that the sole is a bit thicker on this one." He paused from his explanation, taking the time to point out a minor defect, 100 percent unidentifiable by someone not trained on x-ray analyzing. The man shrugged indifferently.

Peter continued. "When this happens we need to search the area." Pause for a B/B/B laugh. Continue. "Unfortunately, that's going to mean cutting into the sandal."

Growing concerned, the passenger said, "I don't have any other shoes. You can see that it's just one piece. How could I have added anything?"

I have to hand it to the passenger, it was in one piece. A normal, run-of-the-mill, non-bomb, one piece sandal. Peter didn't think so. The great thing about Peter is that he's confident in his idiocy. And by great, I mean the worst thing about Peter. He asked me what to do. I said clear it, stop bothering the passenger. He asked the next closest person and they said the same thing. There was no supervisor around, but we can all guess his response, well because he's normal and normal people don't cut up someone's solid sandal, clearly showing nothing other than .005 mm of extra rubber on one. Guess what Peter did?

Pulling a large Swiss Army knife out from the drawer, Peter laughed then mumbled something I couldn't hear, although I assumed was along the lines of, "I'm a big dumb idiot, dadadaddadadad, ahhhhhhh." He carried it to his search table and held it in front of the passenger. He B/B/B laughed again. The passenger made that face you do when you're refraining from murder.

Peter announced, "Let the surgery commence," a statement void of: (prepare yourself) sensitivity; knowledge of what surgery is; awareness of social cues, norms, customs, that we all hate him, the necessity to eat healthy, what constitutes as the actions of a mad man ... I've become lost, let's get back to the story.

I honestly thought some divine interruption (or at least, an adult with common sense) would intervene in the process— didn't happen. Knife tip met yellow, rubber sole and crumbs fell to the bin. Twist, scratch, repeat.

B/B/B laugh, then, "Guess there wasn't anything in there after all," and another B/B/B laugh. The sandal was Swiss cheesed out, unwearable. Peter handed it back. The passenger remained motionless and death-stared him, summoning up his best, *Men That Stare At Goats*, attempt. Unfortunately, it didn't work. Peter remained alive, barely if his abused arteries had anything to do with it. Lopsided, the man left, literally wearing one sandal.

Peter tilted the bin over a garbage can and knocked loose the remaining sandal pieces. The sandal he placed next to the garbage bin, either to preserve it for the passenger in case the dumbest fashion trend ever sparked up on their 400 metre walk to the plane and they came back to get it, or to immortalize the most jack-assed search, decision, and execution I'd ever witnessed. My guess is that his brain didn't think that far ahead, pausing after seeing crumbs and concentrating all its mental prowess on figuring out how to eat a box full of donuts as soon as possible.

Let's go through the remainder of this man's trip. He was on a connection, meaning he still had to go through customs, wait for a plane, get on a plane, land in his destination, take transit to a hotel or resort, and then go someplace in one sandal to buy a replacement. His best case scenario still involved going through customs (possibly the most stern, no nonsense people you come across in your life) with one shoe, then go into an airport shop with one shoe, and purchase a pair of over-priced footwear while wearing one shoe. Meanwhile, Peter gets to chill the F out and eat donuts. Something just doesn't seem right.

# DELAYED FLIGHT

I've detailed my stance on the position of randomizer, so I'll digress from making unflattering ape, human comparisons again. However, I do have another story of being stuck there—this time during a passenger rush and, more importantly, while I was hungover. I'm pretty sure that passengers know when I'm hungover. Questions get dumber. Complaints are more common. Their stupid angry voices are louder. When I can, I disappear when hungover. Unfortunately, I can't use explosive diarrhea to vanish everyyyy day. It's one of those once every few week excuses.

Around six in the afternoon on a Sunday, about the exact time I wanted/needed/was prepared to jab a pen deep enough into flesh that I'd require stitches, for a break, the line for the domestic gates grew huge. We're talking out of the queues and down the hall, big. I hate when this happens. I know what you're thinking, "Wow, that's sweet of you. You really care about the passengers making their flights and not having to wait in long lines."

Wrong!!

I do not care in the slightest whether people catch their flights. The jerk-wad ones anyway. I hope every kind old-lady gets to her plane with time to spare, maybe even a first class upgrade. Everyone else can take a bus, for all I care. No, why long lines bother me is because it's sure to postpone my break—and hungover, the last thing I want, is to be denied my break. I need grease, and lots of it.

Everything was going decently, all things considered. People barely bothered me, probably sensing I'd bite their dicks off if they did. I wasn't getting the usual, "How long is it going to be from here?" then five minutes later, "How about from here?" mumbo jumbo. All of a sudden a couple appeared on my right, seemingly out of thin air.

I turned to them and asked, "Excuse me, did you just skip the queue?" The man, dressed in a Carlton Banks getup, scowled, the way someone with a real Gucci purse would if you asked them if it was fake.

When the left side of his face finished looking yanked by an invisible string, he dick-headishly replied, "Yes. We aren't waiting in that," while pointing at the line.

Entitlement, ugh.

"Why exactly is that?" I asked.

"Have you seen how long it is?" He turned to his wife, then looked back at me, then turned to her again, and said, "Pathetic, just pathetic."

I ignored the pathetic comment; our conversation hadn't reached the combative state where I felt I needed to. Instead, I responded, "Yeah, I'm standing right here. Unfortunately, I've been looking at it for over an hour, but that may change soon."

"Sorry?" he spat. "What do you mean, that may change? Are you implying you'll physically move us?"

Of course, I meant I was about to verbally batter the line butters, saying what every passenger they rudely bypassed in line wanted to say to them. He was a frail fifty-something-year-old and looked millennial psyche breakable; there was no way I'd risk physically moving his porcelain ass.

Me, looking all militant in my uniform, arms crossed, hot buns crossed: "Oh, nothing. So you know that line is for everyone, right?"

Passenger, looking all 'Leave it to Beaver'-face more creased than an NHL net: "Yeah, but we aren't everyone. We'd never wait in that line."

I calmly retaliated, "You ARE actually exactly part of everyone." Getting philosophical, I finished with, "In a greater sense, we alllll are."

He scrunched his face, giving a Haaaaaa what??-look, that suggested he thought I was high. In fairness, I may still have been from the night before.

"Listen, we are not going to the back of the line. My wife is a very important person in this city."

I responded, "I honestly don't care if your wife is that adorable dog I love from 'America's got Talent', you need to wait in line like everyone else."

Outraged, he asked, "Are you comparing my wife to a dog?"

I whispered, "You wish."

Reeling in a state somewhere between confusion, anger, and exploding, he eventually chose to respond with what to him, I assume, was logic. "But we have a flight to catch."

A FLIGHT TO CATCH??!!! A FLIGHT TO CATCH??!!!

*WAVES HIS HANDS LIKE A CHILD DOES WHEN MOCKING. OHHHHHHH. EVERYONE'S GOT A DADDY FREAKIN FLIGHT TO CATCH, PENIS BEND!!!

I repressed my thoughts, semi-conscientious of the repercussions to ejaculating them: An involuntary visit, unpaid, with Big Brother.

With as much subtle condescension as I could muster, I asked, "What do you think everyone else is doing here? Do you think they are confused and waiting in line for Starbucks?"

Running his eyes down, then back up my body, he took me in with disgust. Finally, he proclaimed, "You're very rude." He sucked his teeth and repeated himself. "Very, very rude." He then rolled his eyes towards the ceiling and asked, "Now, which line should we join?"

Was that extra rude his trump card? The kick to the dick insult punchline he'd knock me to the ground with and win the audience's applause? This was a rap battle son! Second "very" was weak sauce; grade six diss.

I slowly pivoted, observing the open doors and their shortening lines. I paused at each one; giving the impression I was going to let them join one. I was not. I swung my hand across the facade, mockingly hesitating at each open door until finally, I violently swung it to the back of the queue, some hundred feet away. I punctuated my dramatics with, "That line!!" announcing the dictation like a deranged game show host.

*The crowd goes wild!!! Mouths form in O's. "Oh's," escape those O's.

The pretentious passenger spat, "Not happening, rent-a-cop."

OH NO, HE DIDN'T!!!

He and his wife took a few steps towards a line. What they didn't know was I'd devised an ingenious, transcending... nay, a monumental method to stop them in their tracks.

"SIR," I sharply spat. "If you don't go to the back of the line, I'm pressing the alarm and saying you threatened my life. What's it going to be?"

Murderous stares, more appropriate for the killer of a family member, locked on to me. I couldn't care less. I didn't budge. They gave in. The two sulked to the back of the line like children being sent to bed early. The person meant to be first in line thanked me, even labelled me a hero. I didn't need his gratification, although it was nice to know someone knew I was a hero.

Oh, and despite my mediumistic efforts, I didn't avoid that meeting with Big Brother.

# C.S.I. (COCK SPECIAL INVESTIGATIONS)

I typed "Big black dick" into Google. The week before I'd typed in "Micro penis", a few weeks prior "penis head bumps". To a dick detective, I'd seem confused about my penis's identity. This may be the case, but not the reason for my large cock search range. "Micro penis" was strictly out of curiosity.

My friend Allysa told me about a guy she'd gone on a few dates with. Even though they'd been drunk and she'd made advances towards his dick, he'd pushed her away. Confident in her game, she told me he was probably a micro penis.

"Micro penis!!?" I asked. The word new to me, it sounded like a cute version of those normal sized, gross penises I'm accustomed to seeing. I pictured the dick version of a Polly Pocket, Micro Machine or miniature pony.

For some reason, Allysa knows a ton about micro penises. One's first assumption would be that it's because she has one, but I've seen her genitalia up close and I'm pretty sure she doesn't. If she does, she's a hermaphrodite. While going down on her, I never noticed a discernible dick tip, definitely no little balls.

She listed TV shows and documentaries she has seen about micro penises. She told me about experiences and near experiences, she and friends had had with the teeny-weeny. I couldn't believe the prevalence of something I never even knew existed and I grew more fascinated every second. I thought back to anytime I might have potentially seen one, however, didn't fully register it as a micro penis. The first thing to come to mind was a few older Asian men's dicks, before basketball in the U of T change rooms. I always tried to look away quickly, but sometimes the nubs stayed in my peripheral, little acorns determined to enter my memory bank. Because of the brief viewings, I can't ascertain whether the dongs and wangs were micro penises. I do remember the pubes being really long. Maybe they just caused a cock-optical illusion. I remember bush acting as a vivacious forest, the penis barely poking through to see the light, a little, shiny, pink mushroom tip, tentatively poking its head out.

My new obsession with micro penises leaves me upset I didn't take the opportunity when I had it. I could have observed them closer, taken a few secret pictures with my phone, candid memories captured for future scrutinizing. The way the older men sauntered around lifting legs and pushing hips forward during dry-downs I could have the world's largest, micro penis photo collection (largest micro penis collection: oxymoron?) by now. Allysa would then revel at my micro penis knowledge, instead of vice versa. The dick bump search was over dick bumps, no big deal; these things happen. It cleared up, I'm all good.

Arguably, the most questionable of the three searches maybe: "Big black dick". Seeing as I'm a white heterosexual male with arguably a medium-sized dick, what would compel me to make the search? I searched it because of an investigation at work into whether I pissed into an alcohol cleaner spray bottle, of course.

I first became aware that I was suspected of being the pee bandit after Jazz approached me and said, "Piss in any bottles lately?" I had no idea what he was talking about.

I answered, "Of course," then walked away.

Later, a supervisor friend elaborated. "Dude, why'd you piss in a spray bottle?"

Once again I answered, "Of course," and walked away.

He caught up to me and told me that anyone who'd been seen in a private search room the day before was being investigated. Someone had peed in a bottle then left it in the room. Someone else had taken it and used it to clean their hands.

Once he'd explained, I said, "This hand washing has been brought to you by the letter P." I'd been in the room for a few seconds to get a Band-Aid. All my pee had stayed in my body while in the room.

The alcohol bottles are used to clean work stations, more or less everyone uses them. I'm not sure if the guilty party had devious intentions or just had to piss really badly. In either case, they were misdirected. The bottles all look the same; there was no way to distinguish the pee bottle from any other. This means your victim could be anyone, including yourself. The risk of being caught in a small room with either your flaccid penis or dangling labia hovering naked over an open bottle, couldn't justify the reward of someone that you may not know possibly spraying diluted pee on themselves. As for having to pee really badly, the washrooms are twenty metres away.

It wasn't until a few days later that I was told by a supervisor friend that I needed to meet with HR. He approached me and said, "You need to go see HR."

"Oh probably," I responded.

"No, I'm telling you, you do have to."

Casually, and with one eye on a female passenger wearing jean shorts so tiny her dirt star was in jeopardy of making an appearance, I continued, "Yeah, I'm not surprised."

My supervisor asked, "Do you know what for? Are you even paying attention? This may be serious."

I pondered the question, scratching my chin for dramatic effect while watching the fading bum of a female with daddy issues or the problematic medical condition of a spontaneously growing arse. Finally, I answered, "Could be anything."

In agreement, he agreed and responded as such with, "You're right. Okay, let me know when you get back what you're in trouble for this time."

On the way to my meeting I ran into the HR person scheduled to interview me. He was standing in line at a Wendy's. We locked eyes a few metres from each other. Through a voice short on breath, he said, "I'm just grabbing a salad. Did you want to meet in my office in ten?"

I shook my head, sternly closing my eyes in slow motion. I responded, "I've got everything I need to do this right here," before holding up my phone.

"What you need? Why do you need anything?" He looked concerned. My Johnnie Cochran impression was having my desired effect; intimidation.

I continued with my confident lawyer routine, offering, "My evidence to exonerate me from this crime." With worry draped on his mug, he responded, "Oh no. We better sit down."

In his baggy, outdated suit, the twenty-eight year old HR representative, Lance, looked more like a fifty-five-year-old, over-weight, and divorced car salesman. We sat down at a two person table next to the Wendy's fast-food kiosk.

"Do you know why you're here?" he questioned. I was

about to ask him the same, but rolled with the conversation. "I believe it's because I've once again been implicated in pee crimes." He didn't know what to say. He sat quiet for nearly a minute. I was using an interview technique I'd heard Barbara Walters mention. Simply be quiet, and eventually your guest/ interrogator will crumble through nervousness. Finally, and with apprehension smeared on his words, he tentatively asked, "What pee crimes have you previously been implicated in?"

I began, "That's neither here nor there." I opened my phone and went to a saved web page. He looked like he wanted to question further, but was experienced enough with me to know the outcome it would have: nada. I continued with, "Lance, before we proceed, I'd like to present you with exhibit A."

I turned my phone and showed him a picture I'd taken of one of the spray bottles. I zoomed in on the nozzle. "If you'd please remember that image." I pulled my phone back, then turned to my second photo. Once again I showed him a picture. This time a big black dick.

"Now, if you take a good look at this picture of my penis ... " He interrupted me to say, "God, dude. What the hell?"

I asked, "Would you like me to zoom in?"

He pushed back in his chair, swivelling his head to protect at least half his melon from the picture. Scrunching his face in the way you do when changing a poop diaper, he defensively spat, "Eww!! No. Get that away from me. Why are you showing me that?"

"That Lance, is a picture of my penis. If you compare the two photos you will see there's no way I could have possibly peed in that bottle."

Still with his face cocked to the side in retreat, he said, "That's not your penis."

I had him right where I wanted him. The jury was about to shift. "How can you be so sure?" I asked sharply. "Do we need to have a meeting with HR about you sneaking peeks while I pee?"

Lance hunched forward, draping himself over the table, lessening the distance his proclamation about perving had to travel. Whispering, he explained, "I've never watched you pee!!"

My voice raised to proclaim, "Tell it to HR!!"

Lance made hush hands, calming down the air before saying, "Let's get back on track here. Are you saying you didn't do it?"

Sliding my chair back and standing, I answered, "I don't need to say anything; the evidence speaks for itself. If the dick don't fit, you must acquit!!"

He looked at me, sighed, sat still for a minute, then said through a surrendered sigh, "Okay, that's all. Let me know if you hear anything about it." I shook my head in agreement, gathered my evidence and left the courtroom ... Wendy's.

# ALL NINE LIVES

F our friends and myself try and go away for each other's
birthdays each year. All five occupy a different month and
spread out, more-or-less, evenly. My birthday is in January and
because it's cold in January where I live, I try and plan my get-
away for somewhere warm. This year, I chose Nashville, Tennessee.

Because Nashville's unwritten slogan is, excess, I came
back worse for wear. Just to indicate how debauched the trip
was, I'll write a brief story that happened before we even
landed; a tale indicative and foreshadowing of the rest of my
birthday weekend.

Our server paused in front of our rowdy group, raucous-
ness enveloping our table, mid-airport bar. She smiled with a
tentativeness that indicated she had something to say that she
didn't think we'd enjoy hearing. Ten beers deep, I had my suspicions what that may be. Ten beers deep, that suspicion lin-

gered somewhere between where thoughts are processed and thoughts are registered, in my head.

"I've been told I can't serve you guys anymore," she administered with downcast eyes.

Collectively, we mocked outrage. We still had an hour before our flight. You'd think that since we were full-bore into drunking, we'd have been dejected by the result. Not the case. My airport is large, full of places to get after it. As we walked away, we pretended our drinking was done.

"Boy, oh boy," I began, still in earshot of the server. Drunk and loud, nearly everyone in the terminal was probably within earshot. I continued, "I sure learned my lesson about drinking too much in an airport. Let's go grab a coffee and sober up, lads."

At the next bar we crushed a couple more, got cut-off again, and with a lengthy five minutes until boarding, found someone else to serve us yet another few.

"Anonymous Author, I'm gonna blow if I don't piss right this minute."

I looked at Ron, his six-four, three-hundred-pound frame spilling over our small airplanes seats and into the aisle and my seat. It would be Niagara Falls up in that bitch if things started spouting off. Despite the fasten-seat belts sign being on, I stood up and motioned for the flight attendant to come over. She shook her head and made a face more appropriate for someone who'd punched her dog in the dick. I more frantically gestured the, come over here, motion. She jabbed her finger like she was scolding me.

"Sorry big guy," I apologized. "She's not having it."

"Too bad. I can't hold it."

He stood up. She gestured for him to sit. He motioned towards the toilets. She gestured more profoundly. He began speed-walking down the aisle. Everyone on the fifty-person plane was watching, enthralled in the drama.

A crinkling on the plane's intercom interrupted the tension, followed by, "Sir, if you don't sit down, there will be disciplinary actions taken." Was she planning to spank him? Throw him out the door?

"I'm going to piss my pants if I don't go now," trailed behind a stampeding Ron.

"BAAAAAAAAAA," pierced the cabin. A red light lit up over the toilet stall just as Ron arrived. He tried to pull it open but couldn't.

"It's locked," she said into the intercom, smugly finishing the fact.

Desperate, he once again yanked, this time using all his force. The door flung open and he entered. When the seat belt light turned off twenty minutes later, you guessed it, our groups' request for beer were ignored.

Immediately after getting back from the trip, I started having sick symptoms of dizziness, nausea and confusion; think vertigo. I'd spent so much money on Jack Daniels, beer and Jack Daniels in Nashville that I couldn't afford to miss work, forcing me to push through.

The first couple of shifts I toughed it out, ending up laid out on the floor trying to find my balance and composure. Usually, the feeling went away after a couple hours, but a hint remained. At the worst times, I'd be disoriented and really have no idea what was happening. It's pretty easy to see how this is problematic at a job where you're required to "stop terrorism". For anyone who's had Tylenol 3, you'll know the plight. I was restricted to tunnel vision and dulled senses. I almost vomited on a former Prime Minister. That bad.

A couple days after the symptoms began, I was working at the front of the line. The position's responsibilities include a prepared greeting (I won't even get into the annoyance of regurgitating this a billion times a day ... yet); scanning passengers' boarding passes and telling them what they need to divest. It's about as simple a job as you'll find paying fourteen pound an hour. Usually, I'm ninety-eight percent asleep, as I recite the procedures. At the very least, I'll fall into a spaced-out zone, droning the required speech. Since passengers don't really listen, it's not overly important I answer their questions with the appropriate answers.

"Yes, you have to take off your shoes," will suffice to the question, "Can I bring this water." Like I said, no one is listening.

So there I am, scanning boarding passes, saying hello etc., like a mindless moron, when suddenly a passenger up and "Pssts" me. Traditionally, pssst isn't an acceptable way for one adult to gain the attention of another adult. "Hello," and, "excuse me," work. Though, I'm out to lunch at this point. I may as well be in a straight-jacket at the nutter house, just staring at paint, wishing someone in a white coat would come and roll me close enough to lick it.

"Yeah, what ... I mean hello ... etc., yeah what's up?" The guy looked sketchy, like he was a car horn's honk away from ripping off his clothes and streaking through a middle school.

Holding his hand over his jibs, the man explained, "I need to talk to you in private," hiding his mouth like a timid Geisha. I took a deep breath. I've dealt with his type before and know a clear mind is essential for repressing my actual thoughts and words to these people. I cautiously began, "Sir, I can't really leave my position to talk to you in private. How about we just whisper, I'm sure no one is listening or cares."

He responded, "It's a delicate situation. I'm not sure how other people will react if they hear." Panic brewed. These aren't words airport security agents want to hear. I thought bomb. Then I thought "Which one of these people will make the best shield if this guy has a bomb?" I tested the waters. "Um, should I be worried about this delicate situation?"

His tone and composure changed, I assume, because I'd jolted him into awareness that his implications suggested his underwear maybe more TNT than FOTL, to someone meant to stop that type of thing. His face lit up with awareness over his words implications. Quickly, he shovelled, "Oh, gosh no. No, it's just weird," towards me.

I focused on his appearance, beginning with his sloppy hair, moving past his poorly groomed mug, down his small-town-living outfit, and finally arriving at a pair of shoes, bright-white with newness. His clothes were hideous; items that when you see them you can only think, why were these made? Like whoever designed them was probably immediately shot. Although, since the looms were already strung and knitting thimbles fingered, the decision was made to finish them. Other than poor fashion sense, he seemed normal enough. Satisfied my life wasn't in jeopardy, I proceeded, saying, "Okay good. So what's up?"

He timidly drew my eyes to a cat cage that was tightly gripped in his right hand. I didn't have to see it there when he first pssst me, to know he had one. Based on his clothes and dishevelment, it was obvious he'd be hauling around a cat. How else could his looking like cat piss be explained?

His cheeks bunched up under his eyes and his head slowly began involuntarily nodding. He explained sheepishly, "I have a dead cat with me", midway through what I thought maybe a stroke. I gave him the exact look you give someone with a dead cat in their hands, telling you they have a dead cat in their hands.

"Um, why?" I asked.

Logically, he explained, "Well, he died ..."

I cut him off and said, "Actually, on second thought, let's not implicate me in whatever is going on here."

"So what do I do?" he pressed."

"I think it goes without saying that you could start by not being so icky."

He nodded in agreement then asked, "Do I carry it?"

Unsure, I offered, "I've never had someone bring a dead

187

cat through, so have no idea. I'll go ask."

I can't imagine there's a dead cat, carry-on luggage prece-dent and I wasn't taking the required steps to find out if there is. The situation was the perfect opportunity to put as much room between cat killer and me as humanly and felinely possible. Also, my break was coming up, I had an idea.

I yanked a passing co-worker by his work shirt and ex-plained, "Yo, Dave, I've got diarrhea. Can you cover me for a hot second while I go tell the supervisor?" I didn't wait for an an-swer, walking away from an unhinged jaw, cooperating with a memory privy of my excuse, prepared to say no.

I approached my supervisor with my best "I'm upset and confused" face. Through near-orphan sadness, I said, "Hey Jus-tin, there's a guy with a dead cat on my line. He wants to talk to you. I'm super allergic to cats and afraid of people that have dead cats with them, so I'm not going back there. I guess I'll just go on break." I made the delivery with speed, hoping my over-whelming word vomit tricked or overwhelmed him into agree-ing. It did. I left. Who knows what ended up happening with that psychopath and his dead cat.

# PART DUH

I magine your crush. How you think everyone you see at a distance is them. How every smell reminds you about them. How all of your thoughts make your way to them. Now, imagine you watch your girlfriend get banged by Ryan Gosling and Eric Bana within twenty-four hours; not as much fun, is it?

The second time I met Ms. Rachel McAdams, I was again on randomizer. Why was I on that dumb position? I have no idea. It's a waste of my mad bag-search and scanning skills. Never has an employee flicked a discarded water bottle into trashcans with such accuracy and flare. I'm Reggie Miller with more masculine facial hair. Randomizer is for dinks; dinks whose only contribution to the checkpoint is pointing in directions. I ain't no dink. I'm an oversized honey-jar chucking maniac. Put me on bag search nerd faces.

"Which way should I go?" an angelic voice asked from behind me. I spun, shook from my NBA JAM internal highlight real.

There she stood.

"Well hello, Ms. McAdams," I said, glowing with joy. "You can go any way you want."

She smiled.

I continued. "Why, may I ask, are you flying with the common folk? At the very least you should be easing your gorgeous self gracefully through the Nexus line."

She casually smiled and shrugged, then walked away, leaving me once again smitten, now with a new, less blog appropriate daydream in my head.

# UP YOUR BUM AND AROUND THE CORNER

I know that I sometimes come across as negative. In actuality, I don't really mind the job. Yes, the passengers can be horrible. Even more yes, a lot of my co-workers are teetering dangerously close to losing an IQ test to tadpoles. Yet still, it has its moments. To me, the best passengers are usually heading out of country on a trip. They are often young and at least partially drunk. With these people, maybe even more than passengers who can't speak English, you can get away with saying a lot of unprofessional things.

A group of seven clearly lit dudes came through late one Thursday night. They approached the line laughing, wrestling and slurring Joaquin Phoenix on David Letterman's late night show bad. The largest of them, wearing a Heineken tank-top, board shorts and a straw sombrero, announced, "Our friend here wants as much touching as y'all can give him. Only from dudes though. He's a." He paused and looked around before curling over himself in a secretive shell, simultaneously funnelling his hand and holding it near his mouth. In what he thought was a whisper, he said in a normal person's normal voice, "Gay boy." I was working at the metal detector, ten-feet away, and heard the comment as clearly as if he was shouting the bigotry into my ear, inches from my external auditory meatus.

Two of the others, dressed in Heineken tank-tops, board shorts and straw sombreros pushed past bigger drunk guy with a peeling tan, and came through the metal detector, surprisingly beep free. Drunks rarely ever divest right. Actually, I guess the only people who consistently do are: business people; middle-aged women who don't travel a lot and think the punishment for beeping is death; and people who work in the aviation industry—we can't risk the embarrassment. It'd be like if a cop did a robbery and his co-workers arrested him. "Gary? What the devil are you doing? You know we don't rob, don't you?"

"I know guys. I'm embarrassed. Don't mention it to Sarge, he'll have my balls."

"Of course, Gary; but for crying out loud, remember next time."

First drunk guy finally came through, slamming off the side and setting off a sharp beeping.

"Was that me?" he asked.

"You who bounced off the metal detector like a pinball? A duhhhhh. Go back and do it right please."

He laughed then went back.

*Repeat.

On his successful pass, he stumbled over to me conspiratorially.

"Our friend, the fat guy at the back." He pointed to a fat guy at the back. "Is loaded. Can you mess with him please?"

I was more than willing to oblige. I looked around the checkpoint to see where my supervisor was; or anyone else who could get me in trouble. The coast was clear. I asked, "Is anything off limits? Your mate isn't going to punch me if I say really bad stuff?"

"No man. He's cool. He'll think it's funny."

"Alright," I responded. "You asked for it."

Fatty McButterpants walked through the metal detector without alarming. Still, I pulled him to the side. Professionally, I delivered, "Sir, the machine has just detected something on you."

Concerned, he asked, "Really? It didn't make an alarm though."

"This is trouble. I now know you're not only obese, but hard of hearing as well."

His face jolted into shock. I continued. "Now if you will step over here, I'm going to be putting my hand in your bum. I'm pretty sure you've got something hidden up your fat ass."

I know worried when I see it, and he was full-blown. Draped in concern, he made eyes at his friends, I assume with hopes they'd jump in. They were huddled at the end of the line, about ten-feet away, chuckling but pretending not to notice us.

Draped in concern, he asked, "You can't do a cavity search on me, can you?"

Still stern-faced, I responded, "Sir, I can do whatever I want. If you wish, we can do a dick search instead. Those are my favourite."

Now blanketed in concern, he asked, "What's a dick search? I don't want that."

Still stern-faced, I responded, "It's where I search your dick." I let it sink with a dramatic pause. I finished with a well-articulated, "Thoroughly!!"

Feeling the onset of hardening cement smothering his

body three feet deep in each direction, he offered, "No, I don't want that either."

My face grew large and my expression altered into epiphany. Fighting the giggles, I delivered, "I see. You must have a small dick then."

"No, I don't," he spat defensively.

"Prove it."

For a second, his posture suggested he was game. Luckily he didn't. There are a lot of cameras in the checkpoint and I think I'd have trouble explaining why I was inspecting a man's dong in front of everyone. Dick searches are a matter of delicacy, privacy, and above all, love.

"Can I just go in that machine?" He pointed to the body scan machine.

"Yes," I answered. He lit up, ecstatic there was a better option. I let the joy set in for a second, then sprung, spitting, "You can. Then we will go to the private search room and I'll search your bum and dick," quickly. I maintained a robotic drone throughout, giving the impression bum and penis searches were all in a day's work.

The cement was hardening quickly, he was about a minute away from being an Italian families' front and back lawn. Burdened by the assumption he may be gay, Butterpants pushed out, "Honestly man, I really don't have anything. What other options do I have?"

I offered, "I could just take pictures of you naked. For my own private collection," as an alternative, then I winked, then looked down in the direction of his junk. I'm pretty sure it had retreated into his junk cavity.

"Crap. Can I leave and just not fly?"

The guy was willing to miss his flight and re-pay for another, some other time. I was obviously rocking level ten torment.

I continued with, "After the pictures, you can do whatever you want. You can even come live with me," then winked again. He was frightened, like he may just find a way to snap his own neck and end it all. Two of his friends couldn't take it anymore and collapsed to the ground in hysterics. I broke and started laughing as well. He clued in, going through a range of visible emotions on his face before bursting out laughing.

Deflated and hunched over, he jovially said to me, "Holy crap man, I totally believed you. You're such an asshole," while patting me on the back in good nature. He then tightly wrapped my neck in a headlock. The last thing I said to him before he unattached was, "Hey be careful, assaulting an officer will get you a cavity and dick search." His friends thanked me and exited laughing.

# BIG D

I hear, "You're too smart for your job," or a variation of it, nearly daily. I mention this not to brag or as a point of pride, but as a precursor to a hearty rant and, maybe, a few supporting stories. The comment brings to mind mostly negative thoughts on my behalf, as do many comments that many different people in both my work and everyday life feel necessary to make. Lagom is a Swedish word generally used to explain; lagom ar bast (the a's in lagom have a couple googly eyes over them but my keyboard doesn't have those symbols, so imagine.), or translated: the right amount is best. Maybe North Americans should give this a try. The, "I'm too smart for my job," pronouncement seems based on little more than my vocabulary or perhaps confidence in what I say. Little do they know, any word I use over five letters is usually made up, or a mince of a few real words I know exist, but don't know how to properly articulate, or sometimes even know the meaning of, and that without spell-check on my computer I'd be closer to writing in Farsi than

English.

I wonder if they're aware of the self-desperatecation involved in their statement. Are they also too smart for the job in their minds? Do they see me in themselves? There are people I work with who not only haven't memorized some of the common rules and regulations that plague us every day, but somehow in ten years have failed to even create a muscle memory of how to log on or off of the same machines they use every day.

Maybe, "You're too smart to work here," is their way of admitting that they are not smart enough to work here. A lot of them stumble around like human versions of wacky inflatable balloons.

I was working with one such airhead on a Wednesday afternoon. Big D lingered at a passenger's upper, inner thigh during a routine security pat-down. He left the area and moved south to satisfy himself that yes, there was in fact something out of place in the above area.

D, the pat-downer, looks like a guard in a World War 2 concentration camp. He wouldn't be one of the guys who were tentative about performing their torturous tasks. He'd be the lead tormentor, tormenting colleagues for not being treacherous enough. The bulky thug would shrug off blunt murder tools as impersonal and choose instead to use his bear paws. He once told me, "I'm a Trump supporter. I won't tell you why in front of the blacks." The blacks he was speaking of were not present. They may have been imaginary, like his girlfriend. I felt engaging him would only lead to more questions that may somehow make me a co-conspirator in hate crimes.

D stepped back from the passenger and held his hands poised in defence. He aggressively said, "SIR, WHAT ARE YOU HIDING BETWEEN YOUR LEGS?" loud enough for the thirty or so people in the checkpoint to hear.

The passenger had an answer, a logical one at that. "My dick." D's face went a brighter red than his fictional victim's fictional wounds. Where other less severe screeners might have let the man go out of embarrassment, D is thorough, and God bless his soul, still thought he had a job to do.

He called me over and the three of us went to a private search room to inspect the area as per protocol when you think a passenger may have something hidden. I asked, "What's the meaning of you interrupting my tranquility, Big D?" as he led me towards the well-endowed gentleman. He responded, "There's an area of concern I'd like to check on this man." I looked at the fella. He was wearing a tight T-shirt, pants and no shoes. The only two places anything could be hidden were his butthole or penis; I was a fan of searching neither.

"The area of concern better not be his dick or I'm gonna be none too pleased, Big D." D shamefully looked down and replied, "It is."

Whether because he has an IQ lower than a brain-damaged gerbil, or because instead of learning English as a second language he's decided to barbarically mimic it, much the way a monkey may mirror a human staring at it through the glass at the zoo, he's easy to screw with.

"Okay, D," I prepped him with. "When we get in there, I'm gonna take a bunch of pictures of his dick then we can sell them on the internet. If his hog is as big as I imagine, we'll be rich." D stopped dead in his tracks. He turned to me, visibly angry. Racism and staring straight ahead with his mouth open, thinking about nothing are his specialty- not humour.

"We are not going to take pictures of his penis." He paused to read my name-tag, even though I've worked with him for three years. "Greg." We held eye contact for a second. I winked, attempting to make his command seem more conspiratorial. Like the math equation two-plus-two, he didn't understand and winked back. Where my wink was dramatic, his was spastic, like a child attempting the contraction for the first time.

We got into the small enclosure and D requested, "Sir pull

your pants down, BUT don't pull out your genitals." He looked at me as if to say, "Gotcha, Greg. Now you can't take pictures of his dick and make us both rich."

The guy looked at him the way you should look at someone who thinks you may involuntarily pull out your cock in a small room with two strangers dressed militantly, one of which sounds and looks like a human version of an ox. The other having threatened to photograph your junk and sell it on the web, even though anyone with half a brain knows dick pics are frequent and free to those who know where to look.

"I wasn't planning on it," he retorted.

"I was," I mumbled under my breath. I then shook my head in disappointment and put away my phone, acting as if he'd foiled my plan. Neither acted like they heard me but both tensed up the way you do when you're bent over with your pants down at the doctor's and hear the snapping on of rubber gloves.

The man tentatively pulled down his pants. I pulled back out my phone, looked at D, and then nodded, indicating it was dick pic time. He shook his head so hard that a breeze unsettled dust from the floor. I raised my eyebrows a few times, hinting the moment was upon us. He reached towards me, I assume to grab it, playing into my plan.

"Big D, how dare you," I spat while withdrawing the phone from his reach. "Trying to take pictures of this man, and with my phone no less." I peered at our victim, attempting to coordinate mutual looks of disbelief. We were on a different page. His was laden with frustration, demonstrating that he was thinking, "Look at the trouble my big ol' dink got me in this time."

Through the awkward tension, D said, "Alright sir, I'm now going to conduct a secondary search on your genital area. My partner is here to witness the search. Do you have any sore areas I should be concerned about?" I threw my hands in the air and rolled my eyes. "This is your dick witch-hunt Big D, not mine. I ain't witnessing crap. I came for the free cookies. Where the H E double hockey sticks are they?" I turned my head and picked a place on the wall to stare instead of the man's dink and balls.

"So what's the story, Big D?" I asked while still looking away. "Does the guy have a huge horn or is he hiding a python in there? Don't want no mother f-ing snakes on the mother f-ing plane, now do we?"

The man giggled. D, stifled, just sighed.

"Everything is fine here, sir. You're free to go."

I asked, "Is that your medical or personal opinion, Dr. D?"

As we left the room, the man held back a laugh and D held back from dragging me to the gas chambers.

# CONNECTION

As you might deduce, there are a lot of complaints made at the airport by passengers, a disproportionate amount of which are towards me. I've avoided follow-up on quite a few occasions because the complaints are made to supervisors who I'm friends with, have something on, or are just too lazy to make a report. What you really don't want is for the passenger to file a complaint with the governing body (Big Brother). These dinks can take your work-pass away, and no work-pass means no chedda.

If a complaint is made against you to the governing body, you're called into a meeting with two people in management. Next, the complaint is recited and the culprit asked for an explanation. I've benefited in these situations because there's no audio on our security cameras and my verbal tirades are done stoically. So, aside from calling in a lip reader or a third-party witness, it's usually the passenger's word against mine. I've had many of these hearings and in all of them stuck to my guns.

To the question, "What were you saying here?" I answer by the books, "Hello, sir/mam. *Fill in the blank with the SOP. I hope you have a nice flight."

When asked why such a professional response led to such a violent verbal outburst and follow-up complaint, I respond, "Passengers are quite often unreasonable. All I can do is my job, follow the SOP, and act professionally, as I did. I hope you have a nice flight. Sorry, habit."

Extending from these meetings, I've had a few disciplinary actions against me. Nothing serious; just a two-day vacation here, a video on how to speak to people there. My work schedule is changeable online and by agreement with other employees, therefore, any suspension less than four days really does nothing more than move my days off that week. That's if I want to pick up shifts and make up the lost hours. I usually prefer to accept the suspensions and destined free time to write and frolic.

The retraining videos are pointless and don't deviate far beyond what I'm supposed to say from an SOP standpoint. The company has yet to come up with a template to combat anything out of the ordinary. Sitting in an office, far from a checkpoint, the creator of said video has decided every incident is manageable by saying words such as "Thank you" and "Sorry". In reality, they make things worse. I've learned the best way to combat anger and dickishness is authority, much as a stern parent would. The method has landed me in hot water. Fortunately, not in the story I'm about to tell you, though.

"Buddy, come with me. Big Brother wants to talk to you."

I put my finger to my nose, squinted, and hummed; universal think deliberation.

Unconvinced, my supervisor shook her head then responded, "You can't even figure out what you've done this time?"

I continued my think gesticulating.

She asked, "Is this going to take a while? Should I cancel

my lunch plans?"

I continued my think gesticulating.

She sighed as she pulled me by the arm. "Let's go."

Big Brother's offices are fashioned and lit like evil rulers on budgets, offices. On a large desk, commonly found in the shop of a small business with two employees, sit five computers crammed together. For some reason, only one of about ten over-head lights is turned on. Swivel chairs that are worn and wobbly are shoved together, prepared to absorb lazy, bureaucratic asses so far into their own diluted reality that shuffling paper and har-assing employees stopping terrorism over an off-centre name-tag is an honest day's work.

"Take a seat," Shawn, one of only two cool Big Brother em-ployees requested. The determining factors to Shawn's coolness came from the three interactions we'd had in the past.

1. Me: "Hey, how's it going?"

Shawn: "Be better if I was at home drinking a beer."

2. Me: "How was your weekend?"

Shawn: "Great. I drank beer and watched football."

3. Me: "Why are they always doing construction on this airport?"

Shawn: "My theory is that the architect was a ditch-dwelling meth-head so high he couldn't tell his ass from his elbow."

The third interaction solidified it.

I knew enough about these types of meetings to shut up. Any extra information I gave would be incriminating. Let them do the leg work.

DO NOT GUESS WHY YOU ARE IN A DISCIPLINARY MEET-ING!! I REPEAT: DO NOT GUESS WHY YOU ARE IN A DISCIPLIN-ARY MEETING!!

Shawn began, "I'll start by saying you are not in trouble. You were just working on a line where a lady's money went missing. We can see from the video that you didn't take it though, and just want to see if you remember her or anything that happened as she came through."

Anxiety air gushed out my mouth, the force sliding me down the pleather chair. We watched a three minute video of a standard passenger commute through the checkpoint. I didn't really understand my role. Shawn looked me in the eyes and said, "Now, as I said, you're not in trouble. However, can you tell me what you did wrong in this video?"

I jokingly asked, "Shawn, isn't this entrapment?"

He laughed. "I repeat. You're not in trouble."

I took a deep breath; I was going to need it.

"Alright, so first, I'm not wearing gloves which I am supposed to be at all times while on the line. Next, I was talking to the x-ray operator – big no, no. I then go up to the front, flipping bins as I go. I stopped to talk to the front person – also not allowed. I then toss the bins onto the other bins instead of placing them nicely. A passenger asked me a question and I ignored them, returning to talk to the front person, distracting them from telling people what to do next. I walked back over to the x-ray operator, spoke to her some more. She gave me a bag to search and I grabbed it, still not wearing gloves. Instead of taking it down the line and using the computer monitor to confirm the item I was asked to check, I look through it in the middle of the belt. I didn't greet the passenger, ask if there was anything sharp or breakable in their bag or confirm it was theirs. I then returned the bag without confirming the item or speaking to the passenger. I then tossed that bin onto a pile of bins. Unfortunately, I missed and it fell to the ground. I went back to speaking with my x-ray operator. I think that about covers it. Did I miss anything?"

Steve nodded, mesmerized either by my memory, idiocy,

or complete lack of remorse.

"Yep. That covers it. You know what you did wrong so don't do it again."

As my supervisor and I left, he yelled after us, "And Linda, get a leash on this guy, would ya?"

Ascending an escalator outside the offices, I turned to Linda and asked, "That was mentally exhausting. May I take a break?" Her eyes closed for a few seconds, and then slowly opened. Finally, she responded, "I hate you."

"Sooooo?" I continued, hoping a plethora of o's would get me what I wanted. She sighed and walked away.

I needed Armando to know my story; we'd been competing since we'd met with best disciplinary tales. I strolled into a checkpoint (not the one I was supposed to go to after my meeting) and went directly up to him. Still ten-feet away, I could see him laughing, all alone, giving the impression some voice in his head had made a funny joke. Self-conscious that the giggles were about me, I wiped my mouth then ran a thorough scan across my nose assessing for boogers. I tried to see my back, wondering if there was a 'Kick Me' sign on it.

"What's so funny, you little rascal?" I asked, arriving at his side.

"You won't believe what I saw this morning. Get me covered and I'll tell you." A clueless newbie was walking by on their way back from a washroom break.

"Hey, Tim, the supervisor just told me to tell you to cover Armando. He needs to put insulin in his body right away or he'll die; but first, he'll convulse."

Everyone knows watching convulsions is the worst. I had him dead to rights. With the fear of Krishna in his eyes, he sprang from his leisurely jaunt and took Armando's place, not realizing I'm a lying prick.

Armando and I slowly sauntered out of the checkpoint. I'm assuming the supervisor was perplexed, trying to figure out why Tim had landed at front, Armando was leaving, and I was even there in the first place. We picked up our sweaters to cover our uniforms then went to a secluded spot.

Usually, Armando just spits out whatever he has to say right then and there, mostly at extremely inappropriate times. For instance, the time he said, "Yep, poop on my dick," just as he turned and nearly ran into someone auditing him for work compliance: spoiler alert, he failed the audit.

We sat down on designated wheelchair seats. Still exhilarated from my meeting, I said, "I'll go first," then spat out my story.

He asked, "That's it? Pshhh. Now prepare yourself. Are you ready for this?" I nodded, my tongue dangling from my mouth like an excited puppy. If he was still confident after hearing mine, his tale had to be great.

He began, "Alright, good. What I'm about to tell you is classified information. It must not be redistributed without the express written consent of me. Do you understand?"

A tad confused, I responded, "Maybe not. The express part is throwing me off a bit. I'm in need of you to write quickly? Or is something else done express?"

Shrugging off my explanation request, he casually explained, "Neither here nor there. I was playing. Tell everyone. Shout it from the rooftops."

"You have yourself a deal," I responded, relieved of my confusion.

"I got called into Big Brother's office to watch a tape about something I did."

I interrupted to say a much needed, "Me toooooo. How depressing is that dank, windowless hovel they reside in?"

"It's perfect for those weasely slugs, but shut-up, it's story time. So, they made me sit down, one of them on either side of me. They said, do you know what we are about to show you? I'm a smart ass so answered, me doing a good job. They said no, no that isn't it at all. Quite the opposite in fact."

I chimed in with, "I bet you were worried sick."

"Yeah, no. I actually just hoped it was something funny. I wanted it to beat your last professional misconduct story."

I thought about which one he was talking about. There were so many. I asked, "Oh, the lunatic lady on about Heathrow as a country?"

"No, the get to the back of the line Starbucks' one," Armando corrected.

"Ah yes. One of many great professional misconducts I've had."

Armando continued. "So they start the video and I already know what's going to happen. Voila, there it is. Me lifting up a bin to stack it and ... boom goes the dynamite, I label an old-lady in the head and she eats dirt. Lights out."

I became the wacky inflatable balloon man, flaring my arms, snapping in the wind, and finally airing out, "Whaaaaa-aaaaaaaaaaa? Are you even talking about? That actually happened? Why didn't you tell me about it?"

He logically replied, "You've been away. Remember?"

"Alas, you're correct my dear friend. A text over something so monumental would be nice though. At least some express drawn crayon pictures of the incident flown by carrier pigeon to meet me in Cuba."

Armando went along with the nonsense, adding, "I did. They must have got lost along the way."

Denouncing yet another aviation vessel, I replied, "Ugh, unreliable, filthy birds. What happened next?"

"Actually, all three of us laughed. It was hilarious. You can see in the video I feel bad. I even go to help her. She didn't even seem mad," Armando explained.

"Probably a little hard to express anger with a concussion. I'm sure she was having enough trouble figuring out where she was."

He laughed, continuing with, "They told me don't hit any more passengers in the head with bins, then we all laughed again. I somehow walked out of a meeting about me smoking an old-lady in the head with a bin, knocking her to the actual ground, and then laughing about it, without being in trouble."

I smiled, excited to get out there and scream the story from the rooftops.

"You're an inspiration to us all," I recited while patting him on the shoulder and slumping lower in my chair, making myself comfortable for what would be a few more hours in the position. He'd won the story-off but neither of us were losers. The only losers were the people who paid us to be degenerates.

# BYE BYE BYE. BYE BYE

**M**y alarm rang, the noise jostling me from a nightmare. Instantly, my foot caught on a pair of jeans, flinging me forward, jamming my wrist off the side of my couch. At my bedroom door, my poor aim led to jamming the same side of hand off the knob. Bob Marley would have been proud of all my jamming. Still half asleep, my first release of urine missed the bowl completely, spraying off the floor and onto my shins and feet. I half-jogged to my bus stop, only for the bus to fly past two seconds before. By the time I arrived at work, I knew my earlier bad luck was an omen. An hour and a half later, I slunk into a checkpoint, sweaty and over life.

With frantic motions indicative of someone eighteen Pepsi's deep, stuck in traffic, and hoping to catch the red-eye leaving in twenty-minutes towards Power Ball headquarters to collect lottery winnings only collectible for the next twenty-four hours, eight states away, a small, Asian man aggressively bobbed while pointing at his luggage, a few bags back in the search bag cue. 'Oh great', I thought. 'First I involuntarily acquire piss smelling scratch-and-sniff legs, and now this'.

I was working with Adnan, an easy-going, plump Indian recently separated from a man-bun, but still hanging on strong to annoyingly finishing peoples' sentences. We'd both just started our shifts. I was feeling blah—although rambunctious— a lifeguard jogging down the beach in slow-motion to motivational music. I felt like taking the piss outta some passengers.

I calmly asked Jumping Jang Sparrow, "What are you pointing at, sir?"

He answered not in words like a human, but by jabbing his finger harder, like an annoying, socially moronic moron.

"Our trolley?" I asked. Adnan, helping his own passenger, giggled.

Despite wearing a tight, adorable suit, the lil' guy began jumping up and down athletically, getting about as much air as you'd expect from a small, Asian business man.

Judging by his aggression about retrieving his bag, I assumed it to be a fully-functional, hollowed out sex doll, stuffed with gold and the cure for short and AIDS. It was black, standard. While looking at him and smiling, I picked up a box of our blue search gloves, feigning excitement over finding his bag.

Jang frowned, bounded quicker, panted harder, and spat, "There!! There!! There!! It's that one!! Why is it there? Why!? Why!? Why!?"

"One question at a time," I interrupted. "You were asking where to get a good sandwich in the airport before. Now, that question is loaded. First, I need to know what kinda sando ya dig, ya dig?"

"Bag! Bag! Bag!," he insisted.

Pause.

If you're picturing this man to be speaking with a strong Asian accent, you'd be wrong. His childish pleas and gestures were done as English as they come; Ya racist.

Resume.

Adnan finished with his passenger and then moved closer to me. Deciding to relieve his jiggling genitals from constant jolting, I dragged Jang's bag to the search table and scanned it. Marked for search on my screen was a laptop and a straight razor with a blade. I held up the razor and shook my head in disappointment, sadly giving him a, "Tsk, Tsk," as I did.

An onslaught of body movement I haven't witnessed outside of watching octopus orgy porn led to the informative explanation, "Razor! Razor! Razor."

A phonetic smorgasbord that may have continued until our societal continuous contribution to the environments degradation global warmed our asses into oblivion if I hadn't cut him off with, "What is it? What are you trying to tell me?"

"Razor!! Razor!! Razor!!" he continued while reaching towards the bag, extending both arms and half his wee torso over a plastic, three-foot barrier marked with clear instructions and words objecting to just that.

I yanked the bag back and said, "Sir, this bag is being searched. Remain behind the barricade and do not touch it." He wasn't going to be deterred.

"But, razor!! razor!!"

"For the love of all that's holy," I interjected. "I know it's a damn razor and it's not allowed. Stop saying razor." I tucked my mouth into my shoulder, moving towards Adnan and finishing in mumble with, "Or I'll cut your head off with it you little dweeb."

I dug the razor, wrapped in a wet cloth, from the bottom of his bag. I obviously wondered what a Premier league football fan towel, drenched to the point of dripping, was doing tightly wound around a razor, but worried what I'd do to the man if I asked and the answer was, "Razor!! Razor!! Razor!!"

I removed the cloth and found the razor enveloped further, in an envelope.

"Let me help!! Let me help!!" he said, vibrating on the spot. Did this razor hold the cure for stubble or something? Why all the excitement? Can Asians grow enough facial hair that a straight razor is a financially sound purchase?

With my gloves on, I had trouble taking the razor from the packaging. Probably because in no world is a razor meant to be held in the packaging. First, paper ripped. Then, that weird plastic window used, I'm assuming, to eliminate the cost of ink used in printing an address twice – once on bill and the other on envelope – because if not for that, then what? Making claustro-phobic paper feel more comfy?

Still gyrating, he offered, "Help!! Help!! Help!!" Presumably, because he wanted to help remove the razor—not because he needed help. Although, if he did, it was for his compulsive habit of repeating unhelpful words.

"Why are you storing your razor in a telephone bill en-velope, anyways? I hope you don't plan to mail this into Verizon as payment for long distance calls." He searched the room for an answer. One didn't present itself. Abruptly, his fanatic move-ments seized. Strangely, the calm was more unsettling than his constant vibrations. Up until this point, he'd seemed jovial and pleasant. The vibe changed.

In a scene that in the movies would start by Actor A grab-bing Actor B's shoulders and steadying them in order to deliver something meaningful, Jang stared into my eyes and delivered, "Sir, I have to pee so badly. Can we please just wrap this up? Do whatever you have to do."

I didn't skip a beat, responding with, "Now you listen here sir. You can pull it out and pee on your bare feet and shins like everybody else." He appeared to be contemplating my sugges-tion. I tossed the razors and quickly sent him on his way.

Not long after, someone complained about me and I was relieved for what my supervisor referred to as a "behavioural timeout." I texted Armando, "Where you at? I just got put on timeout." I got a text back instantly saying, "I'm in the lounge chillin. Come by. Grab coffees; and your balls."

When I got to the lounge, Armando was Chris Brown girlfriend laid out on the attached lounge chairs, watching something on his phone.

"What up?" I asked.

Without taking his eyes off his talk box, Armando replied, "Nada."

I settled into the spot next to him and asked, "You been into a checkpoint today?"

Armando picked his nose, addressed the booger, then me, and then answered, "Nada."

So, it was a philosophical debate he was after. I pulled out my phone and fired up BrickBreaker, convinced that adjusting my behaviour was expected to be a very long process.

Abruptly, Armando declared, "I quit."

"Me too," I half-heartedly replied.

The next day he wasn't there. Nor the one after that; and by-golly, two years later, he still isn't. Now a homage to Armando:

I used to call you my girl
I used to call you my friend
I used to call you the love

The love that I never had

When I think of you

I don't know what to do
When will I see you again?

I miss you like crazy
Even more than words can say
I miss you like crazy
Every minute of everyday
Girl, I'm so down when your love's not around

I miss you
Miss you
Miss you
I miss you like crazy

You're all that I want
You're all that I need
(You're all that I need)
Can't you see how I feel?
Can't you see that my pain's so real?

When I think of you
I don't know what to do
When will I see you again?

I miss you like crazy
Even more than words can say
I miss you like crazy
Every minute of everyday
Girl, I'm so down when your love's not around
I miss you
Miss you
Miss you
I miss you like crazy

I miss you like crazy
Even more than words can say
I miss you like crazy
Every minute of everyday
Girl, I'm so down when your love's not around
I miss you
Miss you
Miss you
I miss you like crazy

I miss you like crazy

# BORED GAMES

S ome days at the airport are soooo mind-numbingly boring. It reminds me of Sundays growing up. Every week, I was woken by a pounding on my door and a, "Anonymous Author, get up. We're leaving in twenty minutes." Five minutes later, my bedroom door was again assaulted, the countdown diminished. I'd slink to the kitchen, pour some cereal and slowly go through the motions of bringing delicious Cinnamon Toast Crunch to my mouth, hoping my lethargic mood annoyed my mom into leaving me at home. It worked maybe once. Next, I'd make my way down a hall jungle thick with shower steam spilled out from the bathroom, grab my church garb (usually laid out by my mom while I'd been eating cereal) then jump into the shower. My last few minutes of sanctuary were spent in front of the bathroom mirror sculpting then ruffling, then sculpting my stubborn mop.

"Anonymous Author, we're leaving!" bellowed from the front door while open, allowing the loud rev of warming up sounds from my dad's Ford F-150 to echo down the hall and into the bathroom. I added some precautionary goop to my bangs and sprang from the house, passing my mom standing by the front door, there to ensure I didn't try and hang back or throw on a pair of mud-covered Chucks instead of my geeky, patent black, church shoes. The service was the worst.

The church service was essentially, some singing, some mumbling in sentences constructed by Yoda, more singing, a plate passed around slowly growing fuller with envelopes and bills, more singing, a man speaking with inflections of tone that only seem appropriate if something 'Catholic priesty' was going on waist high behind the pulpit, and finally more singing. I'm an adult reflecting back and I still think of it as one of the more boring things in the world. Imagine me, riddled with ADHD and hopped up on a bowl of 1000 grams of sugar, sitting through it. Anyways, that's how boring the airport can be some days. Guess that's a long, unnecessary lead in, but you learned a bit about me, so there's that.

I don't like being bored. I don't think there's time in life to be bored. I do whatever it takes not to be bored. So, I entertain myself. This has led victims of this self-entertainment to regard me as a bit of jag-off dinkus. What do I care? I'm on the floor laughing at the Kick Me sign I just placed on eighty-year-old Aunt Agatha's back.

I was scanning in international mid-winter, a time of year I'm especially susceptible to boredom. As I swabbed hand after hand for random search selections, I got an idea. That idea was patty-cake, or as I realized after Googling it, pat-a-cake, pat-a-cake. But, no one probably knows what that means, so with patty-cake we push forward. Passengers came through and beeped. I motioned for them to place their hands palms up. I initiated the game. One of two responses ensued: laughter or confusion.

When Alice, my scanning partner, got a random select,

I low-fived her passenger and her if she made the mistake of putting her hands out to demonstrate. Down low!! I was never too slow!! An audience of eyes grew, both of people who I'd recently tricked into my nonsensical web of games and other less affronted passengers.

"Hey, cut it out," a man of about fifty spat.

I asked, "Cut what out? I didn't do anything."

I looked at Alice and said, "Told you I could act more childish."

She shrugged in surrender. I think she knew I had it in me all along. I continued my discussion with the scissor advocate.

"Listen, if you do that again I'm telling your manager."

I responded, "I'm gonna tell yourrrrr manager," then stuck out my tongue.

Alice's face went red. My face went red. Scissor Sister's face went red. It was like someone who'd been observed in the midst of a crime had smacked our cheeks.

Sometimes stupid things are funnier when you think about them. What a bold, controversial comment. I back-peddled, knowing how embarrassing explaining sticking out my tongue to management would be—especially if it needed to be done after watching video footage, zoomed in. Despite being my friend, I doubt Alice would bother defending me in *The Case of the Immature Twat Who Stuck his Tongue Out at a Passenger*. A bit wordy a title but a shew-in cult favourite with the Gene Simmons' fan community.

Getting out of the scenario seemed impossible, nay, the sound a horse makes. But, I had a secret weapon, and much like the time I got a hold of my friend's Pornhub Premium user name and password, I used it. I beamed – BMW's ad team, fifty years into an attempt to add a new suffix to their rad nickname, gasped in envy – a smile so warm India Indians wore short sleeves around it. Layers of disdain and anger melted away, leaving a man, a man standing in front of a boy, hoping he could love him.

I don't know why my smile works on people. It's possible my aura shines through bright and positive, anytime my lips shoot upward and yellowing jibs are exposed. Although, it's also possible my smile reveals a vulnerable, sad man, someone deserving of empathy and in need of help, specifically from someone professionally trained to work with the mentally ill.

Yeah, so it worked. My mentally-ill facade exposed and accepted.

Patty-cake proved a failure, not the first time getting handsy had backfired for me – shout out Shannon A in sixth grade.

The next day, I was scanning with a co-worker I'd made friends with a few weeks before, someone who against her objections I have nicknamed Big Red for my writing. The two of us met while scanning, on a Sunday, aka hungover day. Standing next to her I shifted restlessly, bending over to stretch and pull at different limbs, attempting to loosen up.

"What's wrong?" she asked.

"Well," I began. "You know when you do the jackhammer during sex, but you don't stretch, and you're old, and afterwards your legs are super-sore? Yeah, so that's what's going on here."

Flabbergasted, her mouth unhinged, and remained agape for a solid minute. I prepared to explain myself to HR. I'd simply exclude the sex part, pretending I did deconstruction on weekends. I wouldn't need to; Big Red was a raw dawg gangsta. She burst out laughing, remaining chortling dangerously far into giggle-shart territory. On break we hung, worked together the rest of that day and the following, she brought chocolate covered raisins the next, and that was that; friends.

Again, bored, I decided to involve Big Red in my follow-up to Patty-cake. Outside, snow fell, fluttering to the airport's asphalt suicidal, volunteering its life for contrast; white on black street crime. I announced, "I've got an idea."

Big Red ignored me. I have about a million ideas a day; nearly all involve me humouring myself at others' expense. I tried a different tactic, a sure-fire way to draw her attention.

"You know how your kids love that toy?" A ventriloquist of donkey puppets would have more trouble talking out his ass. She sprang to life, shifting from her shielded position a few feet away and moving inches from my face.

"Yes," she radiated. "Did you find out where to buy some?"

I brushed her off with, "Maybe." Her face went confused. "Now listen," I said, implying we might be getting down to the toy business. "You know the game Simon Says?" At the sound of the word game, her chubby cheeks shot upward again. I was taking her on a facial elevator ride.

"Yes," she proclaimed.

"Okay," I continued. "Good. So, what do you think about me playing that with passengers?"

She deflated, and then shuffled back to her spot. Her body-language didn't deter me, Big Red doesn't like to be excluded and Simon Says was a multi-player game.

The first passenger came through the metal detector, a kid, maybe sixteen and angsty. Conducive to my game, he beeped. A group of Slip Knot members on his grubby T-shirt peered at me through frightening masks, while the boy asked, "What?"

"Simon says, 'What, what?'" I excitedly replied. I sounded like a deranged, top hat wearing imp who'd play the role of spirit guide on an acid trip.

"What? ... What?" he replied, obviously confused, although years of defiance practice had left his facial muscles unwilling to scrunch a brow in indication, leaving his stiff and unimpressed.

"Simon says, 'Simon says, what what?'"

Cue an exasperation reserved for pestering teachers and

parents.

Slower, I repeated, "Simon says, 'Simon says, what what?'"

Big Red perked up, a smile coming to life. I was the Jigsaw killer and her chained to a chair, knives hinged to her jaw, and a timer set. Actually, we were just co-workers and me a dink playing stupid games with unwilling participants, still, you get the idea.

"My turn," Big Red asked/announced. "Simon says, go back and remove all metal from your person." In her best puppy-looking-for-adoration-and-acceptance impersonation, she vibrated with excitement, trying to not be obvious she wanted me to notice, although, trying to be so not obvious that I did (did that make sense? She wanted me to notice, however, didn't want me to know she wanted me to know, but was being so obvious about it that I did). The kid shrugged indifferently, went back, removed a belt and leather wrist band, returned, didn't beep, shrugged again, stopped, and moved his eyes back-and-forth from Big Red to me, waiting for further instructions.

Here's the only time having children is beneficial in life. Big Red recognized an opportunity and took it. In my brief moment of hesitation, she sprung, winning a game no one ever wanted to play. Lit up like a Christmas tree on cocaine, Big Red directed punk-rock Peter, "Simon says, you're all clear and can go get your belongings."

Checkmate.

Uno.

Kinged.

I'd like to say the game went on all shift and everyone had fun and loved it, but it didn't and they didn't and they didn't. The hell if I was getting one-upped at my own stupidity. It all goes to show, Simple Simon wasn't a pie-man, he was a moronic airport security officer hell-bent on idiocy named Anonymous Author.

# RE-PURPOSING THE PLAYGROUND

Resisting the urge to call Big Red, Armando Part Deux, or Worse Armando, our friendship flourished. Primarily because psychiatry usually cost hundreds of dollars an hour and I was willing to provide it to her for dried mango and chocolate covered raisins, without invitation and often against objection.

A few days later, Big Red and I were again working together. We were relieved for break and started our walk to the lunchroom. Everything was going as usual: passengers paused in awkward locations, disrupting my path; randoms stopped us to ask questions with answers existing directly in front of them; and Big Red voiced her concern about ... everything. Yes, all was normal. That's until a thin, raggedy man caught our attention. Sprawled out on a children's play area mat, he was straddling the leg of a ... less-thin woman. In his hands was one of her bandaged feet (I only took a quick look, nothing long enough to burn my retinas. What I thought were bandages could have been ugly brown socks or torn up nylons; perhaps loose skin). Her egg-roll legs suffocated Value-Mart purchased jeans, leading the way to a torso perfectly constructed for a commercial role as the Michelin Tire Man. We were off-put at what we saw, although relatively indifferent, and excited to eat.

"Was that guy still sucking that lady's toes when you guys were out there?" a co-worker in the lunchroom asked.

"What the Dickens?" I responded. "That really happened?"

"Yeah, I saw it too," another of the five people in the room chimed in. "We all went out to see." Everyone nodded or said things like, "Yeah, it was disgusting."

The place they used as their lookout was less than ten feet from where the foot fetish freaks were treating hippo toes like chicken fingers.

Over the next few hours, the tale was recounted to me many times. The gist of it being that a man sucked off a woman's toes on a children's play mat in a very public area of the airport. Most of my colleagues' discussions were on whether someone should have interjected, threatened or recommended the toesome twosome break it up.

As the murmur of the incident died down, a fiery, blonde, Polish co-worker of mine flung herself into the x-ray room. "A couple was just hooking up outside the bathrooms in the hall. She was jerking him off," she announced. Collectively the room of ten gasped, percolating ears, eyes and anything else percolatable. We had so many questions, nearly all of them starting with 'why'? Why there? Why here? Why didn't they go into a bathroom? Why are they such sex-craved maniacs they are wanking dank in airport hallways? Etc. We all assumed it was the toe sucking bandits at it again, needing another location to keep things fresh, however, it wasn't. A second witness, privy to the pervy things on the play mat, confirmed it was a completely different couple of voyeurs.

You'd think that two completely unrelated acts of sexual deviancy in a workplace would reverberate for ages; would be the chatter of water-cooler gossip, and would taking on legendary opus form, ending up passed on to new hires as old wisdom. Not at the airport. At the airport, that crap is second-rate news. By the next day it was likely that someone had violently chucked poo at a pilot, cut off their nipples by the Subway or dropped dead in a checkpoint. There's no shortage of death and mayhem. The stories last a day, with a few nonchalant murmurs replayed the day after for people who'd missed the previous shift. Even the disgusting section of the tainted play area mat was forgotten; children were no longer warned they were rubbing their two-year-old chops in foot fungus, toe-jam, and arousal.

# TURD TERRORISM

To support the last story,

As usual, I sauntered into the lunchroom at the start of my shift, said something both shocking and appalling, causing an elderly Eastern European and an Indian woman to pause their routine face shovelling to absorb the words' assault. I ripped my wrinkled work shirt from my bag, chucked my lunchbox in the fridge and made my way to punch in.

As I approached the clock, I instantly ate a stink so harsh I involuntarily shot a hand over my nose. The area smelt like a sewage treatment plant had exploded, eaten itself, and then thrown itself up. Before I could escape and find Febreeze to shoot directly into my nose, my supervisor lassoed me with his words. "Where are you going?" he asked. "I need you on the line. Everyone is taking forever on break."

"No wonder," I replied. "It smells like Big Foot's dick crapped in here. Where I'm going, is to cut off my nose so I can't smell it anymore. Why in all that is holy does it smell like this?"

Shawn the supervisor's face grew red, suggesting he was the one responsible. I scrutinized the dumper of his suit pants for any signs that he was the culprit, as he riffled around his cranium searching for the perfect answer to my question. Finally he had it, and answered, "A woman just came through and ... how do I say this nicely, defecated in her pants. The turds fell out the bottom of the leg."

It wasn't the answer I'd been expecting. I'd thought maybe a dog had crapped, or baby's milk had spilled and gone rotten. A human adult had pooed their pants in a public building rife with toilets? Seemed suspect.

Outraged, I berated him with, "What are you even saying? Why are you looking for a nice way to say a grown woman crapped her pants in public? There's a washroom ten feet away. Better yet, hold it, for crying out loud!"

"Yeah, it's obviously really weird," he replied, seemingly unfazed by my tirade. "She did say sorry before she left."

I wasn't done being outraged, enraged and raged. I spat, "Sorry!!! You were satisfied with that? What?!! She didn't pick up her logs? People even pick up their dog's crap. She could have had the courtesy to do that."

Timidly, Shawn responded, "She left, and then we covered it with a bin until the janitor got here."

I think Shawn knew I wasn't done going loco over the poop. Outraged, I responded, "I would have pushed her head down to the poo and said, look what you did, you bad dog. I'm sorry!!! What?!! Everything just continued to operate as normal? Except a poo was sitting under a bucket, unbeknownst to anyone. They just stepped around it? An employee worked beside it like it was their co-worker? A smelly, slightly wet, brown co-worker? What are you even talking about? This is mad!!!"

He didn't answer, he just shrugged. I took it as my opportunity to leave. Once again, I ranted my way out of having to work, not needing to use diarrhea as an excuse for once, some-

ANONYMOUS.

one else had made that excuse for me.

# NEVER QUESTION
# A QUESTIONER

One evening, I was walking down the hall of the airport in uniform during my lunch break. I was both on my phone and eating an apple. I thought the two obstacles would keep the public from approaching me. I was wrong.

"Sir," a lanky woman—averagely-dressed, average-looking, and of average worthiness of description—addressed me. "Might you point me in the direction of ... " she paused, maybe to think, maybe to give me a place in my story of our conversation to write a line about her pausing, who knows. She nodded. My phone friend asked, "What's happening over there?" I whispered, "Not sure. But I see it turning crazy. Quite frankly, I'm excited."

She continued to nod. The nod wasn't your standard nod, one used to show attentiveness or agreement. It was like watching a woodpecker on crack attempt to head butt an unbreakable water balloon to death. I decided to play along. I nodded.

"What's happening now?" my friend asked, about thirty seconds later.

"Head nodding. A lot of it. My neck may snap. I've gotta go." I hung-up, contributing my full attention to the woman.

Woody and I were standing mid-corridor, a vast space visible for a few hundred feet either way. Coming out of the elevator, my co-worker Jazz squinted perplexed before walking up next to me.

"Whatcha doing Anonymous Author?" he asked, obviously intrigued and confused, and high.

"I think," I began, stopping to take a few deep breaths, the laborious exercise (?) growing tiresome. "I've gotten myself into a classic contest of who can head nod the longest"

Jazz smiled, then said, "I'll play," and began bobbing his head as well, a task easier for him, an Indian ... Two full minutes later – I baby goat you not – Average Woody stopped. Then, in a British accent that didn't exist when we first spoke, she announced, "Well, I'm absolutely positive that's the last time I do that," and walked away.

You'd think Jazz or I would've commented on the strangeness of what had just happened, wouldn't you? We didn't. Jazz stopped too, stretched his neck, then in agreement with her said, "Me either." We went back to work.

It's usually easy to ascertain whether someone's about to vomit a question on you while walking the long corridors of the terminal. Not so easy to predict a head-nod off. It only took me a few shifts working at the airport before I'd concocted methods of avoidance to combat these people, aiming to Dikembe Mutombo them pre-question. It's with good reason. Every day at work, I'm presented with some of the laziest questions I've ever heard, without fail. I'm constantly reminded of the Dave Chappelle skit where he and his friend Chip come across a cop while walking the streets high and ask him, "Which way is Third Street officer?" The police officer, flabbergasted, responds, "Heeeeey ... take it easy, you're on Third Street," before issuing them a warning.

The most obvious place to witness this laziness is immediately outside the airport doors, an area designated for passenger pick-up and drop-off. One minute you're outside enjoying a coffee with a friend, and the next, a person who recently stepped out of cab they specifically ordered to drop them off at Terminal 1, is asking you if you know where Terminal 1 is. "Heeeeey ..." I reply, "you're at Terminal 1. Now move it along." Sometimes on bad days I'll respond by saying, with a slow irritated turn demonstrating displeasure, "Yes," and continue my conversation about how stupid passengers are, with my friends.

I'm convinced that if I am ever in a foreign airport and confused, I will refuse to ask for help. I'd rather die, walking around aimlessly, looking for my check-in counter. Employees will notice me and say, "Didn't that guy walk by squinting at signs looking confused and five pounds heavier just yesterday?"

It's not uncommon for a passenger to stand directly under a sign advertising aisle nine and interrupt my phone conversation to ask where aisle nine is, not once bothering to look for themselves. They're content to disrupt my conversation, avoiding that pesky task of using their eyes and reasoning skills. If I happen to bat down their questions, shush or just plain ignore them, they quite often huff in anger or speak loudly about me being impolite. Me, the person speaking to my dying grandmother (for all they know) on the phone during my fifteen minute break. Not them, the imbecile simply waiting for a family member to check-in, before they can say goodbye then leave.

A couple tactics I've invented to deal with awful question askers can be borrowed and also used against telemarketers and those annoying people on city streets asking you to sponsor a child, donate to doctors overseas, protect an endangered species, or some other self-serving, money-grab scheme.

The first—which maybe not as effective outside your place of employment—is merely to say, "I don't work here." The person's perplexed expression grants you enough time to escape. You may hear a couple, "But ... but ... bu--," as you race out of ear-shot. If you're stupid and stick around to hear where those buts are leading, you will find it's almost always, "But you have a uniform on that says Airport Security" or, "But I saw you working five minutes ago." This isn't important, what's important is you're free to enjoy your break in peace.

Another sure-fire tactic is repeating the person's question to them, again walking away before they have time to register the misdirection. Example. "Where do I check in my luggage?" You may notice this question is missing any and all valuable information. What airline are they flying with? Where are they going? Are they flying today? The question may take thirty minutes to answer. Worse yet, upon attempting to answer, the person will most likely throw in a, "Welllllll," and proceed to add an extra twenty questions your way, like we all do on doctor's visits. In conclusion, simply repeat the questioner, emphasizing, "I," and, "MY." "Where can I check in MY luggage?" or, "Where do I go to board?" It's best to start your escape about mid-sentence, letting the remaining words follow you down the hall and away from the passenger. They won't know what hit em.

For the longest time I thought I knew everything there was to know about avoiding passengers questions. That was until I overheard my friend Maria deal with a few.

Outside of the checkpoint, on our way to Starbucks, a ruffled woman approached Maria and I while holding a baby's bottle of milk at arms' length. "Can I bring this?" she asked. It can be assumed she meant on a plane, but given we were in the public area, a few more details should have been added. I opened my mouth to say, "She'll help you," and then point at

Maria and walk-away, asking her order as I fled, most likely returning with her coffee before she'd heard more questions than Alex Trabek. However, Maria schooled me, instantly improvising quadratic formulas in a grade four math contest.

"Ma'am, I could get you a great price for that on the internet. I know a lot of body-builders dying to get hold of protein rich, fresh-from-the-tit milk."

For once, I was the one shocked into silence.

Surprised, over-whelmed, and torn between calling the cops and cutting off her breast, the lady apologized and left. I stared enviously at Maria, lost for words other than, "Wow. I'm paying for coffee."

# THE LGBT CUE

A skinny, colourful person, sharply bee-lined it from hall-way traffic and lunge-stepped to a halt in my path. For some strange reason, he was wearing a pink hoodie missing its sleeves. On the front was a picture of Snoopy in a cape. Written above it in glitter was 'Super Bitch'. For pants, he wore leggings, which he didn't have the **ass**ets to pull off.

"Can I ask you a questjunnnn" he nasally moaned, never enunciating the question into a question, leaving it flat and drawing out a, "junnnnnn," at the end. I knew the question was going to be annoying.

I scrutinized him in scowl for a few seconds, finally addressing him by saying, "You ignored the fact I'm both eating and talking on the phone, so I'm guessing if I said no you'd ask anyway. So go ahead." The person I was on the phone with laughed.

"Well, I don't know about you." His speech became muted

in my head. I took the break to think, "You obviously don't know about me or you'd know I value my break more than any inquiry you have up to and including, I'm dying; where can I find emergency help." My thought ended in time to hear him finish with, "And that's why you should have gender-neutral washrooms. What do you think about that?" The part I missed was a few minutes long; still, I didn't need to hear it to know what I thought. I thought it was a load of malarkey instigated by a grown man in a sweater both inaccurate in the fact that it compromised its own integrity of making people sweat by missing sleeves and by referencing Snoopy – a male dog – as a bitch. I answered, "I'll inform the owner of the airport of your concern," and walked away.

The topic has been coming up a lot in my life, both in media and personally. I enjoy being an asshole, but more importantly an informed asshole. I've taken to watching and reading a lot about both sides, listening to even the most radical spectrum of either. My personal opinion about the pink Snoopy, gender-neutral requesting, washroom 'person', is that he's an idiot. For many more reasons than the fact that he can enter any of the genderless family bathrooms at the airport, pull down his pants and piss in relative peace. I don't think anyone cares what he calls himself while holed up on top of a bowl of yellow. I'm yet to have someone poke their head over my cubicle wall as I drop timber, laugh then say something like, "You're sitting down to pee ... like a girl, not a man ... in the men's washroom, loser."

Not long after, I was working on the full search line. My friend, Jim, was next to me operating the body scan machine. A guy you'd see at any American college football game walked through and beeped, earning a select from the machine.

I explained, "Sir, you've been randomly selected. You can either get a pat-down or go through the body scanner. What would you like?"

Confidently and at a volume demonstrative that he wanted to be overheard, he said, "I don't identify as a sir. I identify as a woman, a sexy woman." He bent his body and squatted in order to see through the metal detector and back at the divest station. A group of guys wearing Michigan State football jerseys smiled, laughed and smacked each other on the back, while looking in our direction. The motions said, "He actually did it! I can't believe he actually said it." So he wanted to screw around; donuts, wall, pizza, orgy.

I proceeded with caution. "I apologize for assuming your gender. What's your name?"

"Mike."

Mike? Good improvisation skills, ya jackass. At least lie with a gender neural name.

"Okay, Mike. If you could just step into the body scanner please?"

Technically, I'm supposed to offer Mike a pat down from someone of the sex of his choosing, but I suspected that's exactly what the perv wanted, and besides, I had a better idea. He stepped in and I pressed the female body scan option.

"Alright Mike, step out please," I directed. All three of us watched as a generic picture of a female body on our computer monitor lit up in the genital area.

Mock concerned, I shook my head. "Mike, I'm afraid the image is showing that you're hiding something in your genital area. I'm concerned you've placed something in your vagina."

Jim, suppressing a violent outburst of laughter, mumbled, "A bomb-ass pussy."

"Jim, don't," I sternly warned.

I continued, "The next step is that you'll be taken to a private room with two females and stripped. They will then check your vagina for any hidden items."

"Are you f***ing kidding me?" Mike shot.

I shook my head 'no'. Jim was holding himself up on the x-ray machine a few feet away, dangerously close to laughing his already slender ass off.

Mike deflated, caving in on himself before pleading, "I'm a guy, okay. A man. I was joking. Let me go again."

I shook my head 'no'.

"Come on man, ask my buddies." He pointed towards them. They weren't laughing anymore. Now, they were friends with a female who had an IED shoved in her poon.

I shook my head 'no'. He grabbed Jim and pulled him towards the body scanner. "You do it man," he pleaded.

Jim, despite my eye-no's, did as Mike asked. Turns out Mike had a dick. A decent- sized dick. Too bad he doesn't have any balls.

# DIRTY HAIRED
# GREMLIN

People can be mean to me. Oh brother, they can be mean. You'd think a bottle of water held the cure to death the way some passengers carry on. I guess it actually technically does, but whatever, that's not my point. Every once in a while, someone crosses the line and steps into verbal abuse territory. I couldn't be happier than when this happens. Things passengers say don't bother me. I don't know them. I don't care about them. Anyone who's berating or insulting a complete stranger, in my opinion, is a complete asshole. Much like when someone farts, I don't care to listen to the useless air coming out of their hole; unless it's Ron, he's got some hilarious butt-air noises. Most importantly, when passengers say something that qualifies as abuse, I get to press the police alarm and watch them become embarrassed in front of friends, family, and more importantly, people they have to sit beside for the next six hours.

I had a lady come through one day who fit these criteria. She was a nightmare and I hope she trips over her laces and skins her knee. Maybe even gets a run in her nylons early in the day with no way to change them. Here's how things went down:

"Ma'am, liquids over one-hundred millilitres are not allowed. You can either put them in a bag and check it in, mail it to yourself, or I can throw it out."

Mean Lady: "Well I'm not throwing it out. If you think I'm doing that you're crazy."

Me: "Good. We've ruled out one of the options."

Mean Lady: "There are no options, I'm taking it."

Me: "Okay, good. So you're going to check it in a bag then?"

Mean Lady: Looks at people nearby for sympathizers to her outrage. No one is looking or cares. "Are you dumb? I'm not checking a bag. I just waited in line. I'm taking it in my carry-on."

Me: I've lost my patience. The time to be polite is behind us. With feigned enthusiasm, I said, "Aw, that's great news."

She lit up, thinking she'd won. I wasn't finished. "So you have decided not to fly today, perfect. I'll show you how to leave the checkpoint."

Never has a face turned from victorious to hate-filled so quickly.

You wonnnnnnnnnn!!! ... a kick in the dick.

Mean Lady: "You listen and you listen good, you punk ... ." Time to interrupt, because that's what punks do.

Me: "Kinda hard of hearing. Can you repeat that?"

Andy, working next to me, paused from searching a bag. He saw the makings of a verbal assault in the works and wanted in on the action. I was waiting for a, "Do you know who I am?" and here it comessssss.

Mean Lady: "Do you know who I am? If you did, you wouldn't bother me about this shampoo."

Me: "I do know you. You're the lady who's not getting on the plane with a two-litre bottle of Herbal Essence."

Mean Lady: "I am and I will, and when I'm done with you, you won't have a job, you punk."

Me: "Jokes on you, I don't even work here anyway. You've been punked." I pointed towards a wall, pretending there was a hidden camera. She looked. I said, "Psych."

Mean Lady: "What did you just call me? F*&^ yourself." She looked at Andy, also laughing, and said, "F&^* you too. You're a bunch of F8&%ing idiots."

Me: "I'm going to give you a quick little warning. That type of language will not be tolerated. If you continue that way I'll have to call the police."

Mean Lady: "F&*^ you," she spat again. A lady standing close pulled her small child away. "I hope you f*&^ing die. You're f*&^ing punks." She ripped the shampoo from my hands and shoved it in her bag. If I hadn't had gloves on she definitely would've cut me with her talons.

Me: "I'm afraid I have some troubling news for you. I'm about to press the emergency alarm and the police are going to come. You can stay here and wait or you can leave and they will find you. Up to you really."

Mean Lady: "I did nothing wrong you F&*&^t."

Me: "Except a lot of things, plus just now you called me a homophobic slur. I'm thinking the cops don't take kindly to hate crimes."

I walked over and pressed the alarm, lowering my finger tauntingly slow as she watched.

Mean Lady: "(Every mean name and swear in the book. Flared fist. A slamming of the shampoo.)"

The cops arrived shortly after and took her to the side. She yelled at them as she looked at me to point and plead her case. In the background, I slam-dunked her shampoo into the garbage, which set her off further. Thankfully, she was escorted out of the checkpoint and more importantly, not allowed to fly. The justice system does work.

# JACOB!!

"My friend Josie wants me to come on her show to tell stories about dating in the city but I don't want to. I told her about you and the blog and said you may be interested in telling airport stories on air. She read them and wants you on. Can I give her your number?"

This text was the first thing I read when I woke up, a startling clutter of unfamiliar words, organized in suggestion of me achieving a larger platform for musings on my questionable work ethic. I love large platforms; back handsprings can be done on them. I messaged my friend D back right away.

"Yes. Yes. A million times yes," I replied.

The host, Josie and I texted and set up a recorded phone conversation for a few days from then. The night before our call, I had baseball. At baseball, I have a lot of beers. When I have a lot of beers, the following mornings are filled with slurred words, moaning and eye-rubbing. Fast forward to our designated interview time.

"Mmmmm, hello?"

"Hi, Anonymous Author? This is Josie. We're calling for the interview. I'm here with Matt. You ready?"

I squinted towards where a nightstand clock would be. I don't have one, nor have I ever; TV and movies condition me once again. Yet to have my morning leak, I was one fart or cough from tinkling my pj's. However, anxious for my first radio recording, I said, "Yeah," then rolled onto my side and flicked on my nightstand lamp; contracting my peenie tube as light shocked my eyes.

Despite all the things against me, I managed to articulate a quasi-entertaining three minutes, minus saying the word "like" more often than a fifteen-year-old valley girl. What I consider the best part of my story, however, was left off-air, most likely because I fumbled the delivery worse than a greasy-handed FedEx man with Parkinson's. It's the story I generally tell when asked what the craziest thing that I've seen while doing airport security is. Here's the wolf's-head story in its entirety.

I'm working front; the x-ray operator called me over. He asked, "That a bullet?"

I answered, "Does a dolphin blowhole make for great sex?"

Perplexed, he stared back blank-faced. Finally, he responded with, "What? What are you talking about?"

He'd obviously never had sex with a dolphin. I gave up and said, "Never mind. Yes, that's a bullet."

He pressed the alarm, locked the bag in the x-ray chamber and we waited for the cops. They arrived with some airport officials and determined the owner of the bag, a fifty-five-year-oldish man with the look of someone who could and likely had, wrestled a bear. He was obviously American, probably from the south, maybe part-bear himself. He wore camo and NASCAR and had stubble thicker than my pinkie finger.

As authority discussed the bullet and prepared to release the bag, Hillbilly Billy had an epiphany. "Ah, I left the bullet in the head, didn't I gents?"

Head? Bullet? The room filled with suspense. A bulky garbage bag rolled in front of us and came to a stop. Billy reached in and fisted something like a sock puppet. A few seconds and some digging later, his arm emerged, bloody to the elbow.

"Guess I forgot to take the bullet out after I shot that G'damned wolf in the head."

Everyone stood quietly in a shocked trance. This is when I sprang into action and said the line edited out of my radio performance.

"NOOOOO!!! JACOB!!!"

Five men, all of authority and stature (aside from Billy), squinted; confused at my shocked outcry. I realized they hadn't understood my hilarious teen romance movie reference. I decided to help them along. "Like Jacob, from Twilight?? The werewolf? Anyone??" Most shrugged with indifference, the others pretended they hadn't heard.

The adults convened for a decision on whether decapitated wolf's heads in garbage bags were allowed as carry-on luggage. I lingered, dejected, a few feet away. Authority determined they'd let him fly with the severed appendage, his home country could worry about it when he landed. Standing next to a guy declaring a jar of sand at customs, I'm sure the wolf head wasn't the last thing fisted that day. All I can say about the whole thing is, poor friggin' Bella.

I'd told some people at work about the radio performance, although, with a six in the morning air time, doubted anyone had listened. I was wrong. A few minutes after I'd punched in and taken my position on the line, Kobe plopped to a grinning stop in front of me.

"We really don't care about the passengers at all?" he asked. He laughed. I shrugged. He continued. "I think that's more of a 'you thing' from what I remember." I shrugged again, indifferent.

Kobe was referring to a part in the interview where I was asked, "For us nervous travellers, what advice would you give us when going through airport security?" I thought about it for a second, going through different options in my foggy mind. Eventually, I settled on, "Well, what's important to remember is that we really don't care about you. We are most likely thinking about when our next break is, or, how tired we are. Yeah, we barely notice you."

It turns out Kobe and a few other people had recorded the interview then posted it in different work WhatsApp groups of two-hundred-and-fifty people a piece. Throughout the day, screeners approached me, saying things like, "Hey Jim, heard you on the radio." Hey Jim, we don't care huh?" and, "Why'd they call you Jim on that interview?"

I hadn't chose Jim. It was chosen for me. In fact, I fretted more over what alias I'd use than any other aspect of the interview. After the eighteenth hiccupped "Ah," Josie chose Jim for me.

Soon, like the wolf's head story, my celebrity was forgotten. I was once again Budget, or Budgie, or whatever incorrect name my illiterate co-workers were calling me after identifying the first two letters of my name then becoming lazy or distracted. My name is pronounced wrong so often that I've actually begun feeling taken aback when it's not. Usually, the only time it's correctly articulated is made by managers reprimanding me or by passengers trying to create camaraderie or the polar opposite; being condescending. These cases make up the few times I make eye contact with passengers, the exception being attractive females.

# SNIFF, SNIFF, HOORAY

A irports, similar to schools and hospitals, are cesspools for germs. Aids probably didn't originate in monkeys. It was likely caused by a group of kindergartners' collective, lewgie/snot hybrid hawk mingling with elderly ass dandruff, teen spunk drizzle, and middle-aged meno sweat on an airport floor, then licked up by a dog who then licked poo, another dog's dirt star, his owner's face and finally a monkey who banged another monkey who in turn got Aids. If my ex asks, it's also where I got the clap.

Despite being a handsome so radiating my smouldering squint alone looks poised to blast disease, age and germ in its tracks, I'm not immune to illnesses. Nay, reproducing blood cells at inhuman speeds needed to replenish overworked cheeks, flushed consistently from the attention of swooning females, may in fact make me more susceptible. In my five years at the airport, it feels as if I'm almost always sick.

On a Monday, three years into employment, thirty-five years into life, I was sick, helluva sick. I woke up. The day instantly ejaculated a month's worth of icky on me. It started right out of the hopper, a rabbit ramming Sickbury eggs up my ass. I struggled down a walking path I take to the subway, aggressively sucking boogs dangerously close to committing suicide from my nose tip every few steps. I paused, catching sight of what I knew was going to be good. Three cop cars blocked in a large dump truck. Five police officers surrounded a swaying, stout man. I pulled out my phone, anticipating stardom on Worldstar Hip-hop. Tall cop asked the man, "Do you know why we pulled you over?"

Hobbity truck driver responded, "Why you what?" in slur.

Tall cop: "You were driving like you're inebriated."

Hobbit: "In where?"

Tall: "Inebriated. Drunk."

The man shook his head to say no, and then opened his mouth to say words. His throat aggressively quivered like a stork swallowing a large fish. He stumbled towards me, keeled over. I responded like a matador, sidestepping. He vomited in a frozen patch of garden five feet from me. The cops prepared themselves for a DUI arrest; I blew my nose, tucked away my phone, and moved on.

I found a seat on the subway, pulled out a book, prepared a Kleenex, and settled in.

Click-click-click. I glanced over subtly, hoping to find the origin of the noise but to avoid the eyes of some of the subway weirdos; it was too early for that. On a back bench to my right, splayed like it was her living room love seat, was an unpredictable-looking Asian woman of about fifty. Both her feet were bare and up on a seat adjacent. In her hand, she held nail clippers. The nearly vacant seat next to her held a small pile of toenails. I didn't need to catch a whiff to know they stunk. I crinkled my eyes in disgust; it was too much for my subconscious to attempt a repressing of reaction. I went back to reading my book and wiping my nose. I wasn't too worried about her activities. If held at the right angle, my book kept her out of view. It also shielded me from any stray hotshot nail projectiles fired in my direction. I did worry for a man two seats over. Not only was he close, but he lacked shaded peepers or a book.

A couple stops later, a heavy girl in snowman printed pyjama pants stepped on and sat between crazy toenail lady and soon-to-be blind guy. Her outfit advertised her as either a well-prepared narcoleptic, or someone who lives underneath the subway platform. Either way, she had potential for craziness. A minute later I knew for sure.

"MA'AM, YOU'RE GROSS!!" Snowman screamed.

"Put your feet awayyyy!!" I knew her outburst was at least partially for show, and I for one appreciated its production value. She violently scanned the car for camaraderie as she belted out her words. Nada. Not one wise person even looked in her direction.

She stood up, flared her arms, demonstrating an immediate intent to fan the foot stank away. She was more mobile than I'd have assumed given her size and slumbery choice of clothing.

"NO!! NO!!" she barked. "You don't do that in public. NO!! NO!!"

Toenails curled into herself. Her little gardening shoes sheathed her feet nearly instantaneously. Frosty wasn't done yet, she had questions.

"WHYYYYY? Would you do that?? HUH!!? HUH!!?" No answer, as you'd assume.

"Are you going to leave those there, you pig?"

She stopped her fanning to point out the yellowing crescent moons contrasting the red seat fabric. The subway stopped. Frosty got out. I guess she was off to sleep, her bed metres away just below us.

I was left torn. I couldn't side with the screaming winter-lover because her outburst was unnecessarily aggressive and embarrassing for toenails. I obviously don't have to mention why I can't side with toenails. I guess it's best I just say they were both in the wrong and should be locked up somewhere I never have to see them.

I arrived at work in desperate need of a hand sanitizer bath and my mommy to rub Vicks VapoRub on my chest and back. That, and someone to restore my faith in humanity. Unfortunately, the moment I stepped onto the checkpoint floor, my supervisor sent me to cover someone scanning. Attempting my usual banter and jibber-jabber diversion tactics were futile, meaning, the layer of filth I'd accumulated on the subway would remain until break. The only good news to be found was that my line mates were mate mates, one of which I'd mock-mated with.

We settled into our usual routine of gossip and banter. It wasn't long before my tranquility was disturbed by a few clueless passengers ignoring requests and questioning things they know nothing about. I turned into sarcastic me, getting even with games and jokes. A man walked in the door, went through the steps fluently then approached the metal detector. I called him through. Beep.

"Sir, your shoes alarmed. Can you please take them off? Bring them back and put them through the x-ray please."

He started walking through again; he sneezed mid-stride. What's important to know about the sneeze is not the sneeze itself. Sneezes, for the most part, are uncontrollable and unpredictable. What's important is that he didn't cover his sneeze, not even a little bit. Y'all icky, Bro, smeared my face and I took a step back, covering my own face with my arm in the process. He stopped in front of me, assuming I needed him for something else. He sneezed once more, again sans coverage. To my left, Jim and my mate-mate were crinkling their brows and covering their noses in disgust. Again, Sneezy released a violent, uncovered spray of sneeze. I'd had enough.

I scolded, "Sir, please cover your face when you sneeze."

"Don't tell me how to sneeze," he replied angered.

I was outraged. I'd understand the retaliation if I'd told him how to walk or breathe, however, not basic manners. I asked, "Why should we have to shower in the mist of your insides? Even kids know to cover their face when they sneeze. You're going to get us all sick because you refuse to move your hand a foot."

His next look was the "Why I never!!" of a rich, old lady wearing pearls and fur coat. Simultaneously, he rolled his eyes and shook his head, shaking loose all the wrongs I'd done him in calling the sneeze out. Still groaning and upset, he stomped to his bags, sharply glancing at us every few steps.

If there is a lesson to be learned from my day, it's that there's a need for a manners' death squad.

A few days later, still sick, I was again taking the subway to work. Honestly, there's no time that I prefer driving alone over public transit than when sick. I'd been fighting the cold for several weeks. Mostly, it was a one-sided battle, in my favour only when Nyquil coursed through my veins late at night. I purposely took a seat away from the majority of the mostly empty car. No one except a flight attendant sat within ten feet of me. My book was in one hand and a tissue in the other, prepared for combat against my constantly streaming nostrils. Between wipes and blows, I sniffled, as you do. In the corner of my eye I saw a flight attendant glare in my direction a few times, giving me that jerky, judgey eye. I tried to hide any mucous activities by doing them when the subway's breaks squeaked to life, arriving at stops. Still, it was obvious my sniffles, stifled the stewardess.

Two stops from my connection, I gave a sniff. She shot around. I noticed her poised, facing me, but decided to stay focused on my book.

"That's disgusting!!" she barked at me. "Don't do that in public."

I turned methodically; dismissively slow-motion blinked, and then responded, "I have nose cancer. I can't help it."

Her grimaced, jerk-face changed to empathetic. The meat scraps she called a neck went from taut and angered to quivering.

"I'm so ... ... so sorry," she stuttered. "I didn't know."

Revelling in my role of victim, I shamed her with a tsk-tsk head-shake and returned to my book. Apparently, she wasn't so, so sorry enough to hang around a diseased nose, because the next time I sniffed, she got up and moved to the other end of the car.

Anyone who takes the airport express bus knows the routine: it arrives, drops off passengers, and then it pulls off to the side, briefly pausing before coming back around. Everyone who's taken *any* bus knows to wait until everyone gets off before entering. However, this etiquette was ignored by Miss, That's Disgusting. The bus pulled up. It opened its doors. She hopped on, pushing past people trying to get off, including a lady on crutches. The bus driver urged her off. I stood by, giddy she'd been put in her place. I was ready to hopefully unleash a really horrible fifteen-minute ride on her. I hate etiquette breakers.

Although I didn't want to be a Pushy Pete and jostle with the other riders, I stood my ground as the doors opened. Normally, I'll allow the exuberant riders who'll do anything short of carving their names into a chair to claim it as theirs, to get on first, but I had a mission. My size and perfected dirty stares got me on right away. I scanned the bus and found my target. To plan, she'd chosen a seat for two. I sprang into action. I hip-checked a sixty-year-old cleaning lady on her last legs. I nearly climbed over a four-year-old more concerned about catching Pokemon than throwing his bag on the designated rack. I slid in beside my victim right before a confused Spanish man. It was sniffle time.

She couldn't hide her anger. She huffed and snapped her head towards the window. The rest of the bus ride went a little like this: I sniffled. She tensed in anger.

*Repeat eight-hundred and seven times.

We pulled into the airport. I had the aisle seat, which meant I was in control of our departure. I decided to be courteous to every, other, single, last, one, of the other bus riders, wishing them goodbye with deep, mucous sniffs. When we were the last two, I looked at my seatmate and new best friend and said, "It was really nice meeting you. Hope you have a nice day," before taking a big sniff and walking away.

# FREQUENT FLYER, MORE FREQUENT ARSEHOLE

I yanked a heavy bag from a support trolley and slid it onto my search table. I scanned the bin and analyzed the x-ray image. I hadn't yet made eye-contact with the owner of the luggage, but I sensed his demeanour; a looming aura of anger.

"This is your bag?" I asked. He sucked his teeth and replied venomously, "Who else's would it be?"

Get out your GPS, Rover, you're barking up the wrong tree.

Eyes half-closed in annoyance, I softly replied, "Anyone's."

Still on that asshole kick, he spat, "It's obviously mine."

Still on that eyes-half closed kick, I softly replied, "Not obviously."

Meany Mean pants rolled his head back, looked around the whole room for someone compassionate towards his plight, then through exasperation spat, "It's mine okay. Let's go."

I asked, "Go where?" Trying to speed up a man who is in control of the tempo, you've just pissed off, and is an asshole to begin with, isn't a good idea.

He answered, "Get this search over with," while rolling his fingers in a 'get going' fashion.

"No problem," I agreeably agreed. I slowly went through prerequisite questions, none of which I ever ask, unless I am trying to delay and annoy a passenger who is being a dick wad to me. He sucked his teeth thirty times while I recited my speech; a habit I detest and that should be left to dentist combating salivation. For every one of them, I stopped to ask if everything was okay. He mumbled some swears under his breath as I delicately removed each individual item from his bag, gingerly placing them on the table. I knew his type. He wanted to complain. I wasn't going to give him a reason, yet. To be honest, I could tell from the x-ray image that his bag was clear; but what fun would letting him go be?

Meany's rapidly tapping toes gyrated his body to a jittery blur before me. He delivered, "I travel a million times a year and never get searched. Why the hell would I get searched now?" nearly in an epileptic fit.

I didn't answer. He'd lost me at a million flights a year.

"Well? Why?" he continued.

My eyes widened, and I asked, "Oh, that was serious?"

His eyes narrowed and his nose scrunched while responding, "Yeah, obviously. Learn to do your job."

Package passed around, back to the beginning, looking for something to slurp up my beverage without it touching my teeth, and there it is, the last straw.

"I thought it was a condescending, rhetorical question," I commented in contemplation.

Meany retaliated. "Well it wasn't rhetorical. Why the other million times didn't it get searched?"

Logically, I responded, "So it was just condescending and rude?"

Meany agreed, begrudgingly replying, "I guess so. So, why?" Back to back so's like a mediocre garment line.

I'd had it. Lecture time. "You're seriously standing here asking me why you've flown a million times this year and never been searched? A million times in one year? Birds don't fly that many times in a year. Zippers don't fly that many times in a year (ya, I came up with that on the spot. I'll accept a freestyle battle anytime you want, Eminem). It's a preposterous comment. On top of that, you expect me to have some record of all those flights and what happened at airport security beforehand? Like there's some gosh darn universal data base recording your infinite journeys? No one cares about any time you fly; none of the millions."

His volume was down but his persistence stood high.

"So, why this time?"

Flabbergasted, I flabbergasted in my pants.

"Go! Please just go. You can complain about me to my supervisor, he's over there." I pointed to a guy in a business suit. A passenger; not my supervisor at all. He walked over and began to speak. The man gave him a shrug and speed walked away. Dishevelled, the million-flights-a-year man confusedly made his way towards customs, where, I hope, he got a hand put up his bum.

# MY PILOT PROGRAM

The domestic departures area has two entrances at my airport. One is directly above the other, about a thirty-second escalator ride. Not a big deal. Especially since escalators are essentially a magical device, incredible if only for the reason that it makes people who use the stair climber at the gym come off as clueless.

I was scanning boarding passes outside of the lower domestic checkpoint, a checkpoint used for connections and overflow passengers. The job is boring and only gets fun when you screw with people or get to send them upstairs; directing a simple route with elaborate, confusing instructions, if you're a dick. I am.

It got busy. Time to send peeps upstairs. A group approached, I asked, "You guys flying domestic?" They frantically nodded and said yes. I volunteered, "Follow me," guiding them towards the escalator they'd need to take. Simple. Maybe even simple as a dimple, ain't it? You can see that the position is easy for most. I assess a line, or have it assessed for me by a supervisor who feels it necessary to point out what constitutes long (look no further than my ween), then point, yell, lead, the passengers to upstairs, a place with more lines open.

An arrogant pilot, walking by on his way back from a flight, certainly didn't think it was simple. Fully decked out in pilot gear, I caught him in my peripheral observing me. Next thing I knew he was inches from my face, asking, "Why are you sending people upstairs when this area is open?" in that voice that says you think you know more than the person you're talking to. Think choda, the zone between a man's sack and anus. Yeah, that's the tone I'm looking for. In the voice, face, posture and tone of a choda, he asked, "Why are you sending people upstairs when this area is open?"

*Side note: He isn't even a pilot from my city.

*Side note 2: He looked about seventy years into alcoholism.

*Side note 3: I really like side notes.

*Side note 4: Pilots have absolutely no authority over airport operations. Hell, with modern technology they barely have any authority in controlling planes. If brain surgery is being done with computers, I'm sure planes can be flown with them: drones. Airlines know people would freak over pilot-less cockpits, aka cock-less cockpits. Maybe their diminished role in flying, and overall glamorization by the public, accounts for so many of them being twats.

Back to the story.

I replied, "Because it's my job. Why do you think you should be interfering with it?"

With an explanation sloppier than his uniform, he spat, "Because you obviously don't know what you're doing. These people are staying here, not going upstairs."

I explained, "No. No, they really aren't," then paused, angling myself to block him. I then directed more people upstairs. Again he interjected, attempting to speak over my directions. Like women at an abortion clinic, I wasn't having it.

"Don't listen to him," I spoke louder. "He's a civilian impersonating a pilot, impersonating airport security."

His face creased, grew redder, and his mouth opened. I beat him to it. Our exchange turned into a childish game of verbal tug-o-war; confused passengers participating as the rope.

His pocked, piggy face grew an even darker colour of red; a shade of, tomato about to blow.

"Go get your supervisor, right now!!!" he screamed. I smiled. I know what I'm doing. You know, I know what I'm doing. Don't you? No, not you. The guy behind you. Yeah, you. Smiling in the face of livid people gets the worst, or best, response available; but, more importantly for my purposes, on security camera it appears as if I'm being a nice, pleasant guy.

I responded, still smiling, "Naw, bro, not happening. Although, it was him that told me to send people upstairs, so if you'd like, I can bring him out so you can tell him what a good decision he's made."

His face screamed, I'm going to rip your pecker off and shove it through your eyeball, however, he only stood still, his eyes growing squinty and beadier by the seconds. An aneurysm was building. He was on the ropes. My ego yelled in the Mortal Kombat voice, "Finish him!!"

I casually suggested, "Can you mosey along please, sir. You're interfering with both my job, and the most direct path these passengers need to take to get upstairs."

He retaliated, "Someone needs to teach you how to do your job because you obviously don't know how."

Even more casually, I explained, "My job is to scan a boarding pass. The prerequisite is having fingers and ability to squeeze." I led his eyes to the trigger and squeezed, aiming the red light at his heart.

"Check. Check," I confirmed.

5:00 p.m.: it was break time. Light bulbs sparked above my bald dome.

Voila laced my next explanation. "On second thought, let me go get my supervisor. Wait here."

I worked my way through waiting passengers and pushed inside, scanning the room for extra bodies potentially just starting their shifts, then for a supervisor. Check. Check.

I said to the person doing front of the line scanning, "Can you go tell John I need to get covered for break, and that I have diarrhea? I'll cover you."

A second later she came back, walking with another screener.

"I'm covering you for diarrhea?" she asked, while scrunching her face in the way you would if I was doing a diarrhea in your presence.

"Yea," I casually confirmed. "Ignore that guy dressed as a pilot out there. He's just some crazy man pretending to be a pilot." With that I entered the checkpoint and walked past everyone, ignoring my co-workers and most importantly the supervisor my pilot buddy was waiting to talk to.

Printed in Great Britain
by Amazon

57745727R00147